# Life across the Waves

楽しいアメリカ生活

William A. O'Donnell
芝垣 哲夫

photographs by
© iStockphoto.com

音声ファイルのダウンロード/ストリーミング

CD マーク表示がある箇所は、音声を弊社 HP より無料でダウンロード/ストリーミングすることができます。トップページのバナーをクリックし、書籍検索してください。書籍詳細ページに音声ダウンロードアイコンがございますのでそちらから自習用音声としてご活用ください。

https://www.seibido.co.jp

**Life across the Waves**

Copyright © 2016 by William A. O'Donnell, Tetsuo Shibagaki

*All rights reserved for Japan.*
*No Part of this book may be reproduced in any form*
*without permission from Seibido Co., Ltd.*

# はじめに

　学生からアメリカに行きたい、留学したい、さらには、アメリカで生活したい、という声を聞きます。アメリカはもはや日本から遠く離れた国ではなく、行こうと思えば誰でも簡単に行けるところです。しかしながら。現実となると、まして長期にわたってということになりますと時間や費用やさまざまな問題があり、それほど簡単ではないようです。

　本書はそうした学生のために、アメリカに行かなくてもアメリカでの生活を肌で感じることができるアメリカ生活入門書となるように書かれています。もちろん、アメリカに行こうと考えている学生にとっては、アメリカにすぐになじめるようなガイドブックのような役割をも果たしています。

　この本は読み物として楽しめるだけでなく、アメリカに行かなくても生き生きとした、そして、楽しい生活を現実感をもって感じることができると考えています。

　各章においてアメリカで実際に生活をしているような場面が次々と目の前に現れてきます。例えば、アメリカの映画やテレビを観ると、若者が広場でバスケットをしています。アメリカではそばを通りかかった人や、そこですでにバスケットをしている人に気軽に声をかけ、即席チームを結成し、試合を楽しむことができます。これを 'pick-up' games といいます。このような言葉はアメリカで実際に生活しなければ耳に入ってこない言葉です。また、アメリカではピザをよく食べますが、ピザも、New York pizza と Chicago pizza の2種類があります。2つのピザにはどのような違いがあるのでしょうか。このようなことを知っていくと、なんだかアメリカ生活が身近に感じられます。

　本書の英文は読みやすい英語で書かれているので学生が楽しみながら読むことができます。そして、Dialog では留学生同志である Mariko と Carlos が日々の学生生活を語ってくれます。

　学生の英語力を増すために練習問題もそろえました。本書により、学生がアメリカ生活の一端を知るとともに、英語の力を増し、さらに、アメリカや異文化に興味を持ってくれれば著者として大いなる喜びです。

　最後になりましたが、本テキストの出版に際し、㈱成美堂編集部の菅野英一氏に、数々のご助言をいただきました、この場を借りて心よりお礼申し上げます。

William A. O'Donnell<br>
芝垣 哲夫

# 本書の使い方

## Vocabulary
本文を読むためのウオーミングアップです。本文に出てくる難解な単語・語句など予備知識を与えるために出されています。1～5を意味の合っているa～eの中から選択します。

## Reading
平易な英文で書かれていますから、まず一度読んでみてください。そのうえでわからないところは辞書などを使ってください。本文の意味がつかめたらCDを何度も聞き、英語に慣れることを勧めます。

## Notes
難解な単語や語句、そして、文化的な内容などが解説されています。

## Reading Comprehension (True or False Question)
本文の内容が理解できたかどうかを確認する問題です。英語の内容を英語でチェックします。

## Word Sense
英語は単語や語句をばらばらに覚えるのでなく、一つの文章として覚えることを勧めます。何度も文章を繰り返し、さらに暗唱することで、英語を英語的な感覚で記憶できます。

## Dialog
日本人の留学生Marikoと、同じく留学生のCarlosとの会話です。リスニングの後で教室のパートナーと何度も会話の練習をしてみてください。

## Dialog Comprehension
会話の内容が聞き取れたかどうかをチェックします。

## Grammar
見過ごしがちな初期の文法の内容を改めてここで取り上げています、文法の復習に役立ててください。

## 一口コラム
アメリカ生活に関するコラムです。楽しみながら読んでみてください。

# CONTENTS

**Chapter 1**  **Making Friends** ...................................................................................1
  〈まずは友達作り〉

**Chapter 2**  **Renting an Apartment** ..........................................................................6
  〈苦労するアパート探し〉

**Chapter 3**  **Setting up a Bank Account** ................................................................11
  〈銀行口座の開設〉

**Chapter 4**  **Phone and Internet Services** ..............................................................16
  〈インターネットの申し込み〉

**Chapter 5**  **Traveling in the United States** ...........................................................21
  〈旅行に行ってみる〉

**Chapter 6**  **Getting a Car** .......................................................................................26
  〈車を買うのか、借りるのか？〉

**Chapter 7**  **New York City** ....................................................................................31
  〈世界のニューヨーク〉

**Chapter 8**  **Sports in the United States** ................................................................36
  〈スポーツとアメリカ人〉

**Chapter 9**  **The Neighborhood Party (Barbecue)** ................................................41
  〈近所の人たちとバーベキュー〉

**Chapter 10**  **Ordering Pizza** ..................................................................................46
  〈シカゴタイプのピザって？〉

**Chapter 11** **Holidays in the United States** ...................................................51
　　　　　　＜民族色豊かなアメリカの休日＞

**Chapter 12** **Weather in the United States** ..................................................56
　　　　　　＜さまざまな天候＞

**Chapter 13** **Complaining** ..........................................................................................61
　　　　　　＜文句を言ってみたい時もあります＞

**Chapter 14** **Farmers' Markets** ................................................................................66
　　　　　　＜ファーマーズマーケット＞

**Chapter 15** **Volunteering** ..........................................................................................71
　　　　　　＜文化を学ぶためにボランティアの体験＞

**Chapter 16** **College Towns** .......................................................................................76
　　　　　　＜活気あふれる大学町＞

**Chapter 17** **American History** ................................................................................81
　　　　　　＜アメリカの歴史＞

**Chapter 18** **Native Americans** ................................................................................86
　　　　　　＜アメリカの先住民＞

**Chapter 19** **The Government of the United States** .....................................91
　　　　　　＜アメリカの政府＞

**Chapter 20** **Washington, District of Columbia (D.C.)** ..........................96
　　　　　　＜政治の中心ワシントン＞

# Chapter 1

# Making Friends

## まずは友達作り

アメリカでの生活を楽しむには友達をたくさん作ることです。公園やコーヒーショップで会った人、スポーツクラブや学校のクラスメイト、そして教会のサークルなどの仲間たちとも友達になれます。

## Vocabulary

1〜5 と a〜e で、双方の意味が似ているものを結び付けてください。

1. strike up
2. suit
3. religious
4. church service
5. cultural experience

a. 文化の経験
b. 〜を作り上げる
c. 適している
d. 宗教的
e. 教会の礼拝

# Reading

Some people are very good at striking up a friendship. They can make friends with people they see every day during a walk in the park or lunch in a coffee shop. Just find an empty seat in a coffee shop. Then ask the person seated next to it, "Is this seat taken?" That can be the beginning of a conversation.

People may also enjoy making friends with the people they work with or their classmates at school. But, one of the easiest ways to make friends in the United States is to join a club or group. There is one to suit everyone's taste, whether it is sports, cards, travel, art, or you name it. Someone in a club may ask you a question like, "Are you from Japan?" Don't answer with a simple, "Yes." Give more information: "Yes, I'm from Osaka. I'll be here for a year." Don't stop there. Ask a question back: "How long have you been a member of this group?"

Churches are also always looking for new members. Whether you are religious or not, attending a church service on Sunday is a good cultural experience. Someone will surely take the time to answer your questions or even ask you to join.

But be careful. Although the old religions are safe and kind, some of the newer ones will simply want your money.

## Notes
**be good at** 〜が上手である　　**strike up a friendship** 友達を作る
**suit everyone's taste** 誰の好みにでも合う　　**you name it** そのほか何でも

Chapter 1  Making Friends

# Reading Comprehension

英文の内容が適切なら（　）内にT（True）を、そうでない場合はF（False）を入れてください。

1. It is better not to talk to people in coffee shops. (　)

2. You should join a group to make friends. (　)

3. There are few clubs in the United States. (　)

4. People attend church services on Sundays. (　)

5. People at churches are always unfriendly. (　)

# Word Sense

次の英文を完成してください。

1. S_ _ _ _ _ _g up a f_ _ _ _ _ _ _ _p with my new classmate was easy.

2. Madonna's music doesn't really s_ _t my t_ _ _e.

3. R_ _ _ _ _ _ _s people go to c_ _ _ _h often.

4. I a_ _ _ _ _ _d the s_ _ _ _ _e last Sunday.

5. Older r_ _ _ _ _ _ _s are kind to their m_ _ _ _ _s.

## Dialog  *The Art Class*

会話を聞いた後で＿＿に英語を入れてください。

Carlos: Where did you buy that painting on your wall, Mariko?
Mariko: I didn't buy it, Carlos. I painted it in my art class.
Carlos: Have you been taking the class for long?
Mariko: Not really. I started it last (1)_____ to make friends.
Carlos: But how could you make such a beautiful painting?
Mariko: Well, my classmates and I all (2)_____ each other. After class we often even go out for pizza together.
Carlos: That sounds like fun. Can I join the class?
Mariko: Sure! I'll see you (3)_____ 7:30 at the Civic Center.

## Dialog Comprehension

設問に対して適切な解答を選んでください。

1. Where did Mariko paint the picture?  ( )
   a. On the wall
   b. In her art class
   c. In a book store
   d. On the street

2. Why did Mariko start taking art classes?  ( )
   a. To make friends
   b. To eat pizza
   c. To take a class
   d. To take photos

3. Who helps Mariko with her painting?  ( )
   a. Carlos
   b. Her mother
   c. Her classmates
   d. Nobody

4. Why does Carlos want to join the class?  ( )
   a. To learn to swim
   b. To play ball
   c. To meet Mariko
   d. To have fun

5. What time is the class?  ( )
   a. Tonight
   b. At seven-thirty
   c. At night
   d. After pizza

# Grammar

**be 動詞**
be 動詞とは am, are, is の総称です。
be は am, are, is の原型で（〜です）を意味します。

❶ 主語が 1 人称・単数の（I）の場合は am を付けます。
I am a student.

❷ 主語が 1 人称・複数（we）の場合は are を付けます。
We are students. （複数）

❸ 主語が 2 人称・単数・複数（you）の場合は are を付けます。
You are a student. （単数）
You are students. （複数）

❹ 主語が 3 人称・単数（he, she, it）の場合は is を付けます。
He is a student.
She is beautiful.
It is a ball.

❺ 主語が 3 人称複数（they）の場合は are を付けます。
They are college students.

次の 1〜3 を英語で書いてください。

1. 私は学生です。あなたも学生ですか。(are you)

2. 彼女は 10 歳ではありません、でも彼は 10 歳です。(is not)

3. 彼らは日本人ですか。はい、そうです。(Japanese)

### Bulletin board

アメリカの大学の食堂や学生寮には bulletin board（掲示板）があります。そこにはサッカーのメンバーの募集や週末のハイキング、寮主催のパーティーの案内などもあります。友達を作るのに、そうしたものを利用するのもいいでしょう。

# Chapter 2: Renting an Apartment

## 苦労するアパート探し

アメリカでの部屋探しはなかなか大変です。不動産業者に紹介してもらうのも一つの方法ですが、もしそこにすでに住んでいる友人などがいる場合は、その人に手伝ってもらうのがいいでしょう。慣れない土地での契約には注意してください。

## Vocabulary

1〜5とa〜eで、双方の意味が似ているものを結び付けてください。

1. real-estate agent
2. budget
3. recommend
4. deposit
5. contract

a. 保証金
b. 契約
c. 不動産業者
d. 予算
e. 推薦

# Reading

If you want to live for a long time in the United States, you will have to choose between buying or renting a house or an apartment. In either case, you will need a real-estate or rental agent. If possible, it is best to ask a friend to recommend one. A good agent will help you find a place to fit your needs and budget.

The rent of apartments depends on their size, location, and number of bedrooms. So, a two-bedroom apartment will be more expensive than a one-bedroom. If renting, you may have to pay one month's rent in advance, another month's as a deposit to pay for any damage you may cause, and sign a promise called a contract to pay rent for a year or more.

When you move out, the deposit will be returned as long as there is no damage to the apartment. However, you may also lose all or part of the deposit if you do not tell the agent or the apartment owner two or three months in advance. Often the rental agent is paid by the owner of the apartment, but sometimes you must pay. Check carefully before you sign the contract.

**Notes**
**a real-estate or rental agent** 不動産業者　　**in advance** 前もって　　**rent** 家賃
**the apartment owner** = the landlord　大家

# Reading Comprehension

英文の内容が適切なら（　）内に T（True）を、そうでない場合は F（False）を入れてください。

1. You should ask a friend to recommend a real estate agent. （　）

2. Size is not important in an apartment's price. （　）

3. The deposit pays for damage caused before you move in. （　）

4. If nothing is broken when you move out, you will get your deposit back. （　）

5. You can move out anytime without telling the owner. （　）

# Word Sense

次の英文を完成してください。

1. You will n_ _ d a real-estate a_ _ _t.

2. Ask a f_ _ _ _d to r_ _ _ _ _ _d one.

3. The d_ _ _ _ _t will be r_ _ _ _ _ _d.

4. Tell the l_ _ _ _ _d before you m_ _e out.

5. Check c_ _ _ _ _ _y before signing a c_ _ _ _ _ _t.

# Dialog   *Finding a Real-estate Agent*   05

会話を聞いた後で____に英語を入れてください。

Carlos:　Mariko, I'm thinking of moving out of my dorm. How did you find your apartment?

Mariko: It was easy. I used a real-estate agent, Mary Andrews. She really helped me a lot.

Carlos: What exactly did the (1)_____ do for you?

Mariko: Lots! She took care of all the paperwork and even explained how to get my (2)_____ back when I move out.

Carlos: Wow! She must have charged you a lot for all that work.

Mariko: Not a cent. She was paid by the (3)_____.

Carlos: Can you introduce me to Mary Andrews?

Mariko: I'll be delighted to. But she's already married, so don't try to date her.

**Notes** dorm = dormitory 学生寮

# Dialog Comprehension

設問に対して適切な解答を選んでください。

1. Who was Mariko's real-estate agent.  ( )
   a. Carlos was.  b. Mary was.
   c. John was.  d. Betty was.

2. What did Mary take care of?  ( )
   a. A dorm  b. An agent
   c. Paperwork  d. Time

3. When will Mariko get her deposit back?  ( )
   a. This morning  b. When she goes home
   c. Tonight  d. When she moves out

4. How much did Mary charge Mariko?  ( )
   a. Nothing  b. One month's rent
   c. Two month's rent  d. A lot

5. Why shouldn't Carlos date Mary?  ( )
   a. She's an agent.  b. She helped Mariko.
   c. She's married.  d. He wants an apartment.

# Grammar

**動詞の疑問文**

❶ be 動詞の疑問文
be ＋ 主語？
**Are you German?**
あなたはドイツ人ですか。
**Is this your house?**
これはあなたの家ですか。

❷ do (does) の疑問文
do (does) ＋ 主語 ＋ 動詞？
**Do you have this book?**
君はこの本を持っていますか。
**Does she go to church?**
彼女は教会に行きますか。

❸ can, will などの疑問文
can (will) ＋ 主語 ＋ 動詞？
**Can you speak English?**
英語が話せますか。
**Will you stay here?**
ここにいてくれませんか。

次の1～3を英語で書いてください。

1. あなたは中国人ですか。（Chinese）

2. 彼女はピアノが弾けますか。（play the piano）

3. この机を使ってもいいですか。（May I）

**Roommate**

学生寮の1部屋やアパートを2人でシェアすることもあります。ルームメイトとの生活は多くのことを語り合える機会でもあり、英語の勉強にもなります。国籍や習慣が異なっていても、とても良い友達になれることがあります。

# Chapter 3

# Setting up a Bank Account

銀行口座の開設

アメリカ生活で必要なものに銀行口座の開設があります。小切手や Debit Card での支払いのために口座を持つと便利です。日本の銀行がある所もあります。

## Vocabulary

1〜5 と a〜e で、双方の意味が似ているものを結び付けてください。

1. bank account
2. check
3. loan
4. interest
5. service charge

a. ローン
b. 利息
c. 手数料
d. 銀行口座
e. 小切手

# Reading

If you plan to live in the United States for more than a few months, you will need to open a bank account with a local bank. In big cities, there will be plenty of banks to choose from. But their service charges can be very different. So, you should choose your bank carefully. However, small towns may have only one bank.

The main bank services are savings and checking accounts, credit and cash cards, and loans. If you put your money in a savings account, you usually get interest on your savings. You can withdraw or take cash from that account at the bank with your bank book. You may also take out money from an automatic teller machine or ATM with your cash card. Charges on your credit card can also be paid through your savings account. Some other bills can be paid automatically from it. Your family in Japan can also send money to it if necessary.

Checks are convenient for paying some bills like rent and taxes. But you may not need a checking account if all your bills can be paid by credit card or automatic payment directly from your savings account. Most ATMs are open 24 hours a day.

**Notes**
**set up a bank account** 銀行口座を開く　**checking accounts**（小切手振り出しなどのための）当座預金口座　**an ATM (automatic teller machine)** 現金自動預け払い機

Chapter 3  Setting up a Bank Account

# Reading Comprehension

英文の内容が適切なら（　　）内にT（True）を、そうでない場合はF（False）を入れてください。

1. Big cities have very few banks.                              (　　)
2. Small towns always have lots of banks.                       (　　)
3. You will usually get interest on a savings account.          (　　)
4. You cannot get money from an ATM with a cash card.           (　　)
5. Checks are convenient for paying some bills.                 (　　)

# Word Sense

次の英文を完成してください。

1. You will need to o_ _n a bank a_ _ _ _ _t.
2. You may have to write a c_ _ _k to pay your r_ _t.
3. If you need m_ _ _y, you can get a l_ _n from your bank.
4. The bank may pay you i_ _ _ _ _ _t on your s_ _ _ _ _s.
5. Credit card c_ _ _ _ _s can be paid d_ _ _ _ _ _y from your bank.

# Dialog   *At the Accounts Manager's Desk*

会話を聞いた後で＿＿＿に英語を入れてください。

Sandy:　Good morning, Mr. Vaccaro. Please sit down. I'm Sandy O'Brien, the accounts manager.

Carlos: Nice to meet you, Ms. O'Brien. Can you tell me about your savings accounts. I need one.

Sandy: Our savings account offers interest and you'll get a cash card to (1)_____ cash at our ATMs.

Carlos: Will I have to pay a service charge if I use the card outside bank hours?

Sandy: Only if you use it at another bank's (2)_____. Just fill out this account application form. We'll also need a copy of your passport.

Carlos: No problem. I'll bring the completed (3)_____ and my passport back this afternoon.

Sandy: Great! We're looking forward to doing business with you.

Carlos: I think I'll enjoy banking with you. See you again this afternoon.

**Notes** application form 申込書

## Dialog Comprehension

設問に対して適切な解答を選んでください。

1. Who is Sandy O'Brien?     ( )
   a. A waitress              b. Carlos' wife
   c. The landlord            d. The accounts manager

2. What does Carlos need?    ( )
   a. A new car               b. A savings account
   c. Ms. O'Brien             d. Local stores

3. What does the savings account offer?    ( )
   a. Interest                b. Another bank
   c. Prizes                  d. ATMs

4. Why must Carlos fill out an application form?    ( )
   a. Because of business     b. To meet Sandy
   c. To get an account       d. For a passport

5. When will Carlos meet Sandy again?    ( )
   a. Tomorrow                b. This afternoon
   c. Before lunch            d. Outside bank hours

# Grammar

**be 動詞の過去形**
be 動詞の過去形は（〜でした）を意味します。

❶ 主語が 1 人称・単数 am の場合
am の過去形は was
I was a pitcher.

❷ 主語が 1 人称・複数 we の場合
are の過去形は were
We were high school students.
主語が 2 人称・単数・複数 you の場合の are の過去形は were
You were a student. （単数）　　You were students. （複数）

❸ 主語が 3 人称単数の he, she, it の場合
is の過去形は was
He / She was a teacher.
It was a hot day.

❹ 主語が 3 人称複数 they の場合
are の過去形は were
They were happy.

次の 1〜3 を英語で書いてください。

1. 昨日は寒かったですか。(cold)

   _____

2. 彼女は良い女の子ではありませんでした、でも今は良い女の子です。(was)

   _____

3. 10 年前、それらの家は美しかった。(Ten years ago)

   _____

 Bank account

アメリカでの買い物や家賃の支払いなどは、現金よりカードか個人小切手の方が便利です。家庭からお金を送金してもらうこともあります。そのようなときのために、アメリカで銀行口座を開設しておくと便利です。身分証明書（パスポートなど）を示せば口座は開設できます。

# Chapter 4

# Phone and Internet Services

インターネットの申し込み

現代の生活で不可欠なものはインターネットです。学生寮にはWi-Fiが設置されていますが、個人でアパートに住む場合は自分でインターネットサービス会社と契約しなければならいときもあります。

## Vocabulary

1～5 と a～e で、双方の意味が似ているものを結び付けてください。

1. complicated
2. service provider
3. landline phone
4. tablet computer
5. Wi-Fi

a. サービス・プロバイダー
b. 固定電話
c. タブレット型コンピューター
d. ワイファイ
e. 複雑

## Reading

Phone and Internet services in the United States can be very complicated. It is best to decide what you really need and how much you are willing to pay before you visit a communications service provider: a telephone or Internet company.

These days many people are rarely at home and find that a cell phone is more convenient than a "landline" home phone. Landlines are the wires that have traditionally connected phones and computers to a telephone company. But new cell-phone technology now allows us to do the same things without the use of wires.

"Smart phones," laptops, and tablet computers can use Wi-Fi to connect to the Internet and take care of the computer needs of most people. Most universities, libraries, and even many businesses, such as restaurants and coffee shops, offer free Wi-Fi Internet services. Besides giving you free access to the huge amount of information on the Internet, these services allow you to use email to send letters, photos, or even movies to your family, friends or anyone you need to contact.

However, for a business with high-speed computing needs, a landline phone connection will be necessary. It is best to shop around for the services that best suit your needs.

**Notes**
**be rarely at home** ほとんど家にいない　　**traditionally** 昔と同等に　　**allow us to do the same things** 同じ事をすることを可能にする

# Reading Comprehension

英文の内容が適切なら（　）内に T（True）を、そうでない場合は F（False）を入れてください。

1. A telephone company is a communications service provider. （　）
2. Most people are at home day and night. （　）
3. A cell phone may be more convenient than a "landline" home phone. （　）
4. Coffee shops always charge money for Wi-Fi service. （　）
5. Landlines are necessary for high-speed computing. （　）

# Word Sense

次の英文を完成してください。

1. Decide what you need b_ _ _ _e visiting a s_ _ _ _ _e provider.
2. Cell phones are often more c_ _ _ _ _ _ _ _t than l_ _ _ _ _ _e phones.
3. Tablet c_ _ _ _ _ _ _s can use Wi-Fi to c_ _ _ _ _t to the Internet.
4. Some c_ _ _ _e shops offer free I_ _ _ _ _ _t services.
5. It is best to shop a_ _ _ _d for a p_ _ _ _ _ _r.

# Dialog  *At Speed-com Telephone's Service Desk*

会話を聞いた後で____に英語を入れてください。

Agent: Hi, I'm Bob Findlay, Speed-com's service agent. What can I do for you?

Mariko: I'm looking for a cell phone and Internet service provider for my tablet computer.

Agent: In that case, our smart-phone service plan gives you a smart-(1)_____ with unlimited Internet service and free local calls for $55 a month.

Mariko: But how can I get Internet service for my tablet (2)_____?

Agent: That's easy. Your smart-phone can act as a Wi-Fi connection for your computer.

Mariko: That sounds like a great deal, but I'd like to shop around a bit before I decide.

Agent: That's always a good (3)_____. But I doubt that you'll find a better deal than ours.

Mariko: In that case, Bob, I'll surely be back. Bye.

## Dialog Comprehension

設問に対して適切な解答を選んでください。

1. What company does Bob work for?      ( )
   a. Internet                b. Speed-com
   c. Cell phone              d. Smart plan

2. Who needs a service provider?        ( )
   a. Mariko                  b. Speed.com
   c. Bob                     d. Findlay

3. What are free in Bob's company's service plan?   ( )
   a. Phones                  b. Internet
   c. Local calls             d. Providers

4. Why doesn't Mariko buy the service plan now?     ( )
   a. He has no money.        b. Bob has a good idea.
   c. There is no time.       d. She'd like to shop around.

5. When will Mariko come back to buy Bob's service plan?   ( )
   a. If Bob's deal is best   b. After lunch
   c. When Bob goes home      d. If the shop is open

# Grammar

**冠詞（a・an）**
冠詞の a, と an の使い方
不定冠詞 a, an は不特定の一つのものをさします。

❶ a は子音で始まる語の前に付け（一つの）（一人の）という意味になります。
I have a book.
My mother is a teacher.

❷ an は（母音 a, i, u, e, o）で始まる語の前に付けます。
There is an apple.

❸ a, an のさまざまな意味。
He is right in a sense.　彼はある意味で正しい。
You must wait for an hour.　君は1時間待たねばならない。
I practice tennis twice a week.　週に2度テニスの練習をします。

次の1～3を英語で書いてください。

1. わたしの父は先生です。

   _____

2. 彼は30分待たなければなりません。（wait for）

   _____

3. 彼女は週に2回テニスをします。（twice a week）

   _____

Crust

日本のサンドイッチには耳（crust）が付いていません。耳の部分が固いので日本人に好まれないのでしょうか。アメリカのサンドイッチには多くの場合耳（crust）がついています。アメリカ人にとって耳のないサンドイッチは頼りないそうです。

# Chapter 5

# Traveling in the United States

旅行に行ってみる

アメリカは、州により景色も人の雰囲気もずいぶん異なるので、旅行は楽しいものです。鉄道はあまり便利ではないので、長距離バスがいいかもしれません。

## Vocabulary

1〜5 と a〜e で、双方の意味が似ているものを結び付けてください。

1. depend on
2. be reversed
3. custom
4. contrary to
5. passenger line

a. 旅客用鉄道
b. 〜に反して
c. 習慣
d. 〜が逆向きである
e. 〜によって決まる

# Reading

Traveling in the United States depends on your destination (the place you are going), your budget (how much money you can spend), and how much time you have for the trip. If you have an International Driving Permit, renting a car is cheap and easy. But driving laws and customs are different in each state.

In many states, but not all, drivers may turn right after stopping at a red light, if it is safe. Contrary to many countries, people drive on the right side of the road. That can be difficult, because the position of the mirrors, light and wiper controls, and even radio are reversed. Moreover, people from smaller countries are often not used to driving the long distances between cities in the United States.

Only a few big cities like Boston, New York, Washington, D.C., San Francisco, and Chicago have subways and local railroads. Airports are also usually found only near large cities. So, if you want to visit a small town, you will probably have to take a bus or taxi from the nearest city or airport.

Although the United States was once a leader in railroads, now there are only a few major passenger lines run by Amtrak, the national railroad company: one along the east coast and three crossing the country from coast to coast.

**Notes**
**drivers may turn right after stopping at a red light** 赤信号で一時停止した後に右折してもよい　　**Amtrak** 全米鉄道旅客公社

# Reading Comprehension

英文の内容が適切なら（　）内に T（True）を、そうでない場合は F（False）を入れてください。

1. Having an International Driving Permit makes renting a car easy. (　)

2. Driving laws are the same all over the United States. (　)

3. In some states you can make a right turn even if the traffic light is red. (　)

4. Most small towns have big airports. (　)

5. The national railroad company is called Amtrak. (　)

# Word Sense

次の英文を完成してください。

1. Traveling d_ _ _ _ _s on your b_ _ _ _t.

2. R_ _ _ _ _g a car is easy if you have a l_ _ _ _ _e.

3. Some people are not used to t_ _ _ _ _ _ _g long d_ _ _ _ _ _ _s.

4. Amtrak is the n_ _ _ _ _ _l railroad c_ _ _ _ _y.

5. In small t_ _ _s you will have to use b_ _ _s and taxis.

# Dialog    *Taking a Trip*

会話を聞いた後で____に英語を入れてください。

Carlos: Mariko, that suitcase looks bigger than you. Where are you going with it?

Mariko: I'm on my way to the train station to catch the Amtrak to New York.

Carlos: Amtrak? You have an International Drivers License. Why don't you just rent a (1)_____?

Mariko: I would, but the traffic in the city is heavy and New York State traffic laws are different from here.

Carlos: Why not take a plane? From here to New York takes only about an hour, but Amtrak (2)_____ three.

Mariko: Yeah, but getting from the airport to downtown adds another hour or more.

Carlos: I guess you're right. You can relax and read a book on the train.

Mariko: Exactly, and the Amtrak (3)_____ station is downtown right next to my hotel.

Carlos: At any rate, I'll get my car and give you a lift to the station. That suitcase will break your back.

## 🎧 Dialog Comprehension

設問に対して適切な解答を選んでください。

1. How big does Mariko's suitcase look?    (   )
   a. Smaller than Carlos        b. Heavier than him
   c. Older than Mariko          d. Bigger than her

2. Why is Mariko going to the station?    (   )
   a. To rent a car              b. To catch a plane
   c. To take a train            d. For shopping

3. Why doesn't she want to drive to New York?    (   )
   a. The traffic is heavy.      b. The laws are the same.
   c. Her suitcase is light.     d. The rent is expensive.

4. What can she do on the train?    (   )
   a. Wash her clothes           b. Read a book
   c. Work at home               d. Relax in the city

5. Where is her hotel in New York?    (   )
   a. At the airport             b. In the suitcase
   c. Very close to the station  d. Outside the city

# Grammar

**名詞**
名詞にはいくつかの種類があります。

❶ 普通名詞　　(table, doll)　She has a doll.
　　　　　　　(family)　　His family lives in New York.

❷ 固有名詞　　Kenji, Tom, Kyoto, New York
　物質名詞　　milk, water, sugar, salt
　抽象名詞　　love, beauty, happiness, music

次の1~3を英語で書いてください。

1. 紙を3枚ください。(three sheets of)

   _____

2. 浩二は音楽が好きです。(likes)

   _____

3. 私のクラスには20人の学生がいます。(There are)

   _____

### Greyhound Bus

アメリカ旅行に最適なのがグレイハウンド社の長距離バスです。アメリカを縦横無尽に走り、3,100ほどのルートがあります。カナダやメキシコまで行くこともできます。レンタカーもありますが、運転するときには交通規則が州により異なることもあるので、注意が必要です。

# Chapter 6

# Getting a Car

車を買うのか、借りるのか？

学生は自転車やバスを利用する人が多いのですが、車を持つ人もいます。車は新車を買うよりも中古車を買い、アメリカを去る時にそれを売ればいいのです。

## Vocabulary

1〜5 と a〜e で、双方の意味が似ているものを結び付けてください。

1. lease
2. transportation systems
3. include
4. value
5. steering wheel

a. 価値
b. 自動車のハンドル
c. 一定期間借りる
d. 交通手段
e. 含む

# Reading

People who live in New York City or other very big cities have very little need for a car because the city transportation systems usually include buses and subways. But in the rest of the United States, life without a car can be difficult. If you only need a car from time to time for short trips, renting a car is probably the cheapest. Generally speaking, the longer the rental time, the cheaper the daily rental fee will be. But, if you need a car every day, it is better to buy or lease one.

Leasing is like renting, but a bit more expensive, since you must take care of the car and even make minor repairs. If you plan to be in the United States for over two years, you might better buy a car. Then you can sell it when you leave and get back some of the money you spent on it. In that case, it is often better to buy a slightly used car than a new one, because used cars are cheaper and lose less value over time.

Taking your car back to your home country can be very expensive. Besides, if the steering wheel there is on the right, your American left-hand steering wheel may make driving difficult.

### Notes

**have very little need for a car** 車の必要性はほとんどない　　**from time to time** 時々　　**the longer the rental time, the cheaper the rental fee will be** 長く借りればそれだけ安くなる　　**lease one** 車をリース（賃貸借）する　　**lose less value over time** 時間がたっても価値はほとんど下がらない

# Reading Comprehension

英文の内容が適切なら（　）内に T（True）を、そうでない場合は F（False）を入れてください。

1. If you live in a big city, you must have a car. 　　（　）

2. The longer the rental time, the cheaper the daily fee will be. 　　（　）

3. Buying a car is a good idea if you will be in the United States for several years. 　　（　）

4. Over time, used cars lose less value than new ones. 　　（　）

5. Taking your American car back to your home country is definitely a great idea. 　　（　）

# Word Sense

次の英文を完成してください。

1. Jack l_ _ _ _d a new car for two y_ _ _s.

2. W_ _ _ _ _ _ _ _n, D.C. has a good t_ _ _ _ _ _ _ _ _ _ _ _n system.

3. John b_ _ _ _t a car that i_ _ _ _ _ _d not only a radio but even a TV.

4. New cars quickly l_ _e a lot of their v_ _ _e as soon as they are first used.

5. Taking an American car back to your home c_ _ _ _ _y can be e_ _ _ _ _ _ _e.

# Dialog　*Getting a Car*

 13

会話を聞いた後で____に英語を入れてください。

Mariko: Carlos, I'm tired of waiting for buses. I'm going to get a car.

Carlos: I bought my car used and it was pretty (1)_____. You could do the same.

Mariko: Yes, but you're good at fixing cars and I'm not. Besides, I want a new car to take home to Japan.

Carlos: Bad idea! American cars have their steering wheel on the (2)_____.

Mariko: Well, then I'll sell it before I leave to get back some of my money.

Carlos: That's possible. But a new car loses value as soon as it's driven.

Mariko: What if I lease a car. Then I can pay while I'm using it and just give it back to the (3)_____ company when I go home. I'll check it out.

Carlos: If you need any help, don't be afraid to ask me.

## Dialog Comprehension

設問に対して適切な解答を選んでください。

1. What is Mariko tired of waiting for?  ( )
    a. Trains              b. Buses
    c. Taxis               d. Planes

2. Who is good at fixing cars?  ( )
    a. Mariko's father     b. Carlos' friend
    c. Carlos              d. Mariko

3. Which side of the road do Americans drive on?  ( )
    a. The left side       b. The inside
    c. The right side      d. The outside

4. What does a new car lose as soon as it is driven?  ( )
    a. Its steering wheel  b. The keys
    c. Its driver          d. Much of its value

5. When can Mariko pay for a leased car?  ( )
    a. The next day        b. While using it
    c. Before driving it   d. Before New Year's Day

# Grammar

**名詞の複数形**

❶ 数えられる名詞には s を語尾に付けます。a pen（単数）　pens（複数）

❷ 語尾が s, ss, ch, sh, x, o で終わる語には es を付けます。
bus (buses)　class (classes)　bench (benches)　dish (dishes)
box (boxes)　potato (potatoes)

❸ 語尾が（子音字＋y）で終わる語には y を i に変えて ies を付けます。
baby (babies)　lily (lilies)　story (stories)

❹ 語尾が f, fe で終わる語には、f, fe を v に変えて es を付けます。
wolf (wolves)　knife (knives)

❺ 不規則に変化するものを不規則変化といいます。
A) 母音を変える　　　　man (men)　tooth (teeth)
B) en. ren を付ける　　ox (oxen)　child (children)
C) 単数・複数が同形　　deer (deer)　sheep (sheep)　fish (fish)

次の 1〜3 を英語で書いてください。

1. 私は羊を 2 匹飼っている。(keep)

2. 君には歯が 2 本しか残っていません。(have, two teeth left)

3. 彼女には 3 人の子供がいます。(has, children)

 **Jack-O'-lantern**

10 月 31 日のハロウィーンにはカボチャのお化け Jack-O'-lantern（ジャック・オー・ランタン）が登場します。カボチャをくりぬき、夜にはろうそくを入れ、怪しげな光が出るようにして窓辺に置きます。

# Chapter 7

# New York City

## 世界のニューヨーク

ニューヨークは何と言っても世界の中心地です。入植したオランダ人によって創設された後、世界の人々が集まる大都市になりました。世界の文化・経済の中心、ニューヨークを見てみましょう。

## Vocabulary

1〜5 と a〜e で、双方の意味が似ているものを結び付けてください。

1. population
2. be founded by
3. the Dutch
4. the capital
5. representatives

a. オランダ人
b. 首都
c. 代表者
d. 人口
e. 〜によって創設された

# Reading

With its population of over 8.4 million people, New York City is the largest and many would say the greatest city in the United States. The city was founded by the Dutch in 1624 and came under the control of England as New York in 1664. From 1785 to 1790, it was the capital of the United States. The area around Wall Street, which once housed George Washington's American government, is now the financial capital of the world.

The city is now made up of five boroughs: Brooklyn, Queens, Manhattan, the Bronx, and Staten Island. The center and busiest of them all is the island of Manhattan. But in its center is the peaceful green of Central Park. The park is four kilometers long and almost one kilometer wide, with a lake, several ponds, and even a zoo.

New York City has over 120 universities and many famous museums. Visitors from all over the world come to see plays at its Broadway theaters, visit the Statue of Liberty and Empire State Building, or eat at restaurants in one of its international districts like Chinatown or Little Italy. The city also is home to the United Nations, where representatives of all the countries of the world gather to plan its future and search for ways to make it peaceful.

**Notes**
**the financial capital of the world** 世界金融の中心地　　**once housed** かつて〜が置かれていた　　**five boroughs** New York City の５つの行政区
**representatives** 代表者たち

# Reading Comprehension

英文の内容が適切なら（　）内に T (True) を、そうでない場合は F (False) を入れてください。

1. New York City has fewer than eight million people.   (　　)
2. The city was founded first by the English   (　　)
3. The American capital was once in the area around Wall Street.   (　　)
4. New York has over 120 universities.   (　　)
5. Visitors usually come to Broadway mainly to eat international food.   (　　)

# Word Sense

次の英文を完成してください。

1. Many w_ _ _d say New York is the g_ _ _ _ _ _t city in the United States.
2. After being f_ _ _ _ _d by the Dutch, New York came under the c_ _ _ _ _l of England.
3. Wall Street is the f_ _ _ _ _ _ _l capital of the w_ _ _d.
4. New York has many u_ _ _ _ _ _ _ _ _ _s and famous m_ _ _ _ _s.
5. The city has many i_ _ _ _ _ _ _ _ _ _l districts like Chinatown and Little I_ _ _y.

# Dialog  *A trip to New York City*

会話を聞いた後で____に英語を入れてください。

Carlos: Mariko, I see you're back from your New York trip. How was it?

Mariko: Great! I saw a Broadway play in the afternoon and ate dinner at a festival in Little (1)_____.

Carlos: Isn't that backwards? Usually people go to the theater in the evening.

Mariko: Yeah, but (2)_____ afternoon matinee tickets are half the evening prices.

Carlos: That's a good deal. Did you see the Statue of Liberty?

Mariko: Another bargain. The Staten Island Ferry sails right by it. I took the (3)_____ and it was free.

Carlos: Mariko, you're the best bargain hunter I know. Can I ask your advice on my next trip?

Mariko: That depends on whether you'll take me along?

## Dialog Comprehension

設問に対して適切な解答を選んでください。

1. Who went on a trip?  ( )
   - a. Carlos
   - b. The ferry
   - c. Mariko
   - d. Staten Island

2. Where did Mariko eat dinner?  ( )
   - a. In Little Italy
   - b. On Broadway
   - c. At a play
   - d. In Chinatown

3. Why did Mariko buy a matinee ticket to the Broadway play?  ( )
   - a. It was afternoon.
   - b. She likes Italian food.
   - c. It was half-price.
   - d. It was a theater.

4. What does the Staten Island Ferry sail by?  ( )
   - a. Central Park
   - b. Chinatown
   - c. Little Italy
   - d. The Statue of Liberty

5. How much does the ferry cost?  ( )
   - a. It is free.
   - b. It costs more than a play.
   - c. It costs a fortune.
   - d. A lot of money

# Grammar

**付加疑問文**
話し手が聞き手に同意や確認を求める場合に使う疑問文を付加疑問文といいます。
肯定文には否定文、否定文には肯定文を付けます。

❶ 肯定文には否定文を付けます。
She is a school teacher, isn't she?
彼女は学校の先生ですね。
You went to the park yesterday, didn't you?
昨日、君は公園に行ったよね。

❷ 否定文には肯定文を付けます。
He doesn't play tennis well, does he?
彼はテニスがうまくないよね。
They didn't speak English, did they?
彼らは英語を話さなかったね。

❸ 助動詞も付加疑問分が作れます。
He can't swim, can he?
彼は泳げないよね。
You will stop talking, won't you?
話をやめてくれますね。

次の1〜3を付加疑問文を使って英語で書いてください。

1. 彼女はまだここに着いていないですね。（hasn't arrived, yet）

2. トムは先週、日本へ出発しましたね。（left for）

3. あなたはあの人を知っていますね。（don't you?）

**Free concert**

週末にセントラルパークなどの公園では無料のコンサート（Free concert）が催されます。お天気の良い日曜の朝、公園をぶらっと歩いて音楽を楽しむのもいいものです。公園ではジョギングをしている人がたくさんいますが、これもアメリカ文化の一面です。

# Chapter 8
# Sports in the United States
## スポーツとアメリカ人

アメリカの映画や TV 番組などで、広場でバスケットをしている光景をよく見ますね。アメリカでは、そばを通る人にプレーに入ってくれるよう頼むことができる、pick-up game というものがあります。

## Vocabulary

1～5 と a～e で、双方の意味が似ているものを結び付けてください。

1. professional
2. seasonal
3. public school
4. pick-up game
5. uniform

a. ユニフォーム
b. プロ
c. 季節にあった
d. 公立学校
e. 即席の試合

## Reading

The major professional sports in the United States are seasonal: baseball in spring and summer, American football in fall, and basketball in winter. Some sports, like tennis and golf, are played anytime and anywhere weather permits. Soccer has become popular in American schools but not at the professional level.

For those who would rather play than watch, there are clubs offering every sport. They usually require club membership, uniforms, and fees for use of club facilities. But for those who want to play a sport simply when they feel like it, there are lots of opportunities.

When not in use for classes or games, most public schools open their baseball and football fields to anyone who wants to use them. Small towns and cities do the same with their public playgrounds, which often include tennis and basketball courts. These facilities are generally free to the public or charge a very low booking fee for exclusive use at a particular time.

Any group of friends can start a game of basketball or any sport and add players from whoever happens by and is willing to play. For these "pick-up" games, the uniform is whatever you happen to be wearing.

### Notes
**not in use for** 〜に使われていない    **exclusive use** 貸切

# Reading Comprehension

英文の内容が適切なら（　）内に T (True) を、そうでない場合は F (False) を入れてください。

1. In the United States, most professional sports are seasonal.  (　)

2. Soccer is a major professional sport in the United States.  (　)

3. Sports clubs never require membership.  (　)

4. Public playgrounds are usually free.  (　)

5. You must have a uniform to join a pick-up game.  (　)

# Word Sense

次の英文を完成してください。

1. Many p_ _ _ _ _ _ _ _ _ l sports are s_ _ _ _ _ l.

2. Golf can be p_ _ _ _d anytime weather p_ _ _ _ _s.

3. There are lots of o_ _ _ _ _ _ _ _ _ _ _s if you want to play a s_ _ _t.

4. P_ _ _ _c schools open their playing f_ _ _ _s to whoever wants to use them.

5. A u_ _ _ _ _m in a pick-up game is w_ _ _ _ _ _r you are wearing.

# Dialog  *A Pick-up Game*

会話を聞いた後で____に英語を入れてください。

Mariko: Hey, Carlos, could I interest you in playing a bit of basketball this evening?

Carlos: I haven't shot hoops in a long time so I'm a bit rusty. Besides, I don't have a (1)_____.

Mariko: Uniform? You don't need one for a pick-up game. What you're wearing now will be fine.

Carlos: Then I'd love to play. But who's on the team?

Mariko: There's no (2)_____ yet. I've asked Jack and a couple of other friends. We'll pick sides before the game.

Carlos: Great. Where's the court and how much do we have to pay?

Mariko: We're going to use the court at the public school and it's (3)_____. We're meeting at six.

Carlos: Then count me in. See you then.

**Notes** **shoot hoops** バスケットボールをする　　**pick sides** 2組に分かれる　　**count me in** 私を仲間に入れる

## Dialog Comprehension

設問に対して適切な解答を選んでください。

1. What does Mariko want to do this evening?　　(　)
   - a. Eat dinner
   - b. Have a party
   - c. Play basketball
   - d. Pick up games

2. Why doesn't Carlos need a uniform?　　(　)
   - a. He's rusty.
   - b. It's a pick-up game.
   - c. His uniform is old.
   - d. Mariko has one.

3. When will the group pick sides for the game?　　(　)
   - a. Tomorrow morning
   - b. After school
   - c. While playing
   - d. Before the game

4. Where is the basketball court?　　(　)
   - a. At a school
   - b. In a park
   - c. At a field
   - d. In a store

5. How much will the group have to pay to use the court?　　(　)
   - a. A small fee
   - b. Nothing
   - c. Some money
   - d. It doesn't count

# Grammar

**指示代名詞**
this や that を指示代名詞といいます。
this は比較的近いものを指すとき。
that は比較的遠いものを指すとき。

❶ This is my hat.
これは私の帽子です。
These are my books.
これらは私の本です。
(this の複数形は these)

❷ Is that your brother?  Yes, he is.
あの人はあなたのお兄さんですか。　はい、そうです。
Are those boys your friends?  No, they aren't.
あの少年たちはあなたの友達ですか。　いいえ、違います。
(that の複数系は those)

次の 1〜3 を英語で書いてください。

1. これはあなたのコートです。そしてそれは私のコートです。(mine)

2. これらはあなたの本ですか。(Are they)

3. これは英語の辞書です。でもそれは違います。(an English dictionary)

### New York Mets

アメリカの野球チームの応援は阪神タイガースの応援に負けません。ヤンキースかメッツか、という意見の違いから別れたカップルもいるとか。野茂英雄選手がメッツに入団し登板した時、その美しいトルネード投法はニューヨーカーを熱狂させました。

# Chapter 9
# The Neighborhood Party (Barbecue)

近所の人たちとバーベキュー

アメリカの家庭では、週末にバーベキューをします。近所の人たちを誘ってみんなで楽しむ the neighborhood party があります。

## Vocabulary

1～5 と a～e で、双方の意味が似ているものを結び付けてください。

1. neighborhood
2. host
3. grill
4. show off
5. take pride in

a. 焼き台
b. ～を見せびらかす
c. ～を誇りに思う
d. 近隣
e. 主催者

# Reading

During the summer, especially on weekends, there are neighborhood parties all over the United States. A family will invite their neighbors to a party in the backyard of the house, usually in the late afternoon. The family hosting the "barbecue" will provide charcoal and the barbecue grill, sometimes a fireplace or brick barbecue pit. The neighbors will bring enough food and drinks for themselves, generally with something to share with others: hamburgers, steak, spare-ribs, salads, cakes, or pies.

Everyone helps with the cooking. Even children try their hand at cooking simple foods like hot dogs. However, starting the fire, keeping it going, and grilling the meat is traditionally left to the men, especially the host. Perhaps it is a way for men to show off their cooking skills as the sons of ancient hunters.

The party usually ends in the early evening. The neighbors take turns holding the barbecues and take pride in how many people come and how much fun they have.

Barbecues are a good chance for neighbors, both adults and children, to get together, learn about each other's lives, share local information, and become closer friends. They are a unique part of American culture.

**Notes**
**brick barbecue pit** れんが造りのバーベキュー炉　　**try their hand at cooking** 調理に挑戦してみる　　**keeping it going** 火を燃やし続ける　　**as the sons of ancient hunters** 古代狩猟民の子孫のように

Chapter 9 The Neighborhood Party (Barbecue)

# Reading Comprehension

英文の内容が適切なら（　）内に T（True）を、そうでない場合は F（False）を入れてください。

1. Families invite neighbors to barbecues.　　　　　　（　）
2. The neighbors bring nothing to the parties.　　　　　（　）
3. The meat is usually cooked by the women.　　　　　（　）
4. Neighbors take turns holding barbecues.　　　　　　（　）
5. Barbecues are only a chance to eat good food.　　　（　）

# Word Sense

次の英文を完成してください。

1. People have n_ _ _ _ _ _ _ _ _ _d parties in the s_ _ _ _r.
2. One family h_ _ _s the barbecue in its b_ _ _ _ _d.
3. That family p_ _ _ _ _s the c_ _ _ _ _l and the place to cook.
4. Everyone c_ _ _s on the barbecue g_ _ _l.
5. Families take p_ _ _e in hosting a b_ _ _ _ _ _e.

# Dialog  *The Barbecue*

会話を聞いた後で____に英語を入れてください。

Carlos:　Hey, Mariko, are you going to Frank Sill's barbecue on Saturday?
Mariko:　I hadn't heard about it, Carlos, and Mr. Sill hasn't invited me.

Carlos: It's a neighborhood party, Mariko. We're all (1)_____. Frank wants everyone to come.

Mariko: Do I have to bring a gift or something for the Sill family?

Carlos: Not really. Frank has a barbecue pit in his backyard and everyone brings food and drinks to (2)_____.

Mariko: Fantastic! I'm sure I can put together something everyone will like. What time will the party begin?

Carlos: There's no set time, but a little after three will be good. It'll be over about seven.

Mariko: It sounds like fun, and I'm sure we'll (3)_____ make lots of new friends. I'll see you there, Carlos.

## Dialog Comprehension

設問に対して適切な解答を選んでください。

1. Who is having the barbecue?  ( )
   a. Mr. Sill
   b. Mariko
   c. Carlos
   d. Mariko's family

2. Why should Mariko feel she is invited to the barbecue?  ( )
   a. Sill invited Carlos.
   b. It's a neighborhood party.
   c. Carlos likes Sill.
   d. She likes Frank.

3. What will Mariko have to bring for the Sill family?  ( )
   a. Money
   b. Presents
   c. Nothing
   d. A pit

4. What time should Mariko arrive at the party?  ( )
   a. After three
   b. After seven
   c. Before noon
   d. Exactly at three

5. What sounds like fun to Mariko?  ( )
   a. Lots of food
   b. The barbecue pit
   c. The neighborhood
   d. Frank's barbecue party

# Grammar

**不定代名詞の some と any**
some や any ははっきりとしていない数量・人・物を示します。
どちらも「いくつか」「いく人か」などを表します。
some は肯定文に、any は否定文や疑問文に使います。

❶ some「いくつかの」
He has some old Japanese coins.
彼は何枚かの古い日本の硬貨を持っています。

❷ any「いくつかの」
Do you have any questions?　何か質問はありますか。

❸ [どんな～] でも
Any student knows it.　どんな学生でもそれを知っているよ。
I can't wait any longer.　これ以上待てません。

次の 1～3 を英語で書いてください。

1. 私に手紙が来ていますか。(Are there, for me)

2. もう少しコーヒーはいかがですか。(How, about, some)

3. それを何かの本で見ました。(saw, some)

### Potluck dinner

アメリカ人は頻繁にパーティーをします。そのとき、パーティーの主催者が飲み物から食べ物まで、すべてを準備するのは大変です。そこで、みんなが飲み物や食べ物を持ち寄り、それをシェアします。これを potluck dinner（ポットラック ディナー）といいます。

# Chapter 10

# Ordering Pizza

## シカゴタイプのピザって？

ピザはイタリア移民がもたらしたものですが、今ではアメリカに定着し誰もが食べます。トッピングに何を載せるか考えるのは楽しいですね。

## Vocabulary

1～5 と a～e で、双方の意味が似ているものを結び付けてください。

1. ingredient
2. immigrant
3. crust
4. topping
5. be shaped like

a. ～のような形をしている
b. トッピング
c. ピザの生地
d. 移民者
e. 材料

## Reading

Many foods have entered the United States along with its immigrants. But pizza, which was brought with Italian immigrants, holds a special place in American society. Most restaurant foods are served on plates for individuals, but pizza is made to be shared. When friends go out for an evening or want to sit around and talk after a ball-game, pizza makes the perfect meal: inexpensive, easily shared, and topped with healthy ingredients like cheese, meat or seafood, tomato sauce, and vegetables.

On the east and west coasts of the United States, the most common form is flatbread or New York pizza, with its round, thin, flat crust. In the Midwest, deep-pan or Chicago pizza is popular. Its thick crust is shaped like the long pan it is baked in. Pizzas are usually priced by their width, 9, 12, or 18 inches, plus the type and number of their toppings. The thickness or thinness of the crust and the special mix of toppings is a source of local pride.

Of course, there are nationwide pizza chain stores whose pizzas will taste very much the same in any part of the United States. But true pizza-lovers will always claim that their local pizza shop, or perhaps their mother, makes the best pizza in the world.

In spite of its Italian roots, pizza has become as American as apple pie.

### Notes
**flatbread or New York pizza** 平たい生地のピザ　**deep-pan or Chicago pizza** 厚い生地のピザ　**Its thick crust is shaped like the long pan** その厚い生地は、長いベーキングパン（焼き型）のような形をしている

# Reading Comprehension

英文の内容が適切なら（　）内にT（True）を、そうでない場合はF（False）を入れてください。

1. Pizza is made to be shared.　　　　　　　　　　　　　　（　）

2. Pizza is too expensive for a meal with friends.　　　　　（　）

3. New York pizza is made in a long flat pan.　　　　　　　（　）

4. People are proud of their local pizza.　　　　　　　　　　（　）

5. Pizza was eaten in the United States before in any other country.　　　　　　　　　　　　　　　　　　　　　　（　）

# Word Sense

次の英文を完成してください。

1. Cheese and t_ _ _ _ o sauce are common i_ _ _ _ _ _ _ _ _s of most pizzas.

2. The art of making pizza e_ _ _ _ _d the United States with Italian i_ _ _ _ _ _ _s.

3. Chicago pizza is p_ _ _ _ _r in the M_ _ _ _ _t.

4. The meats or v_ _ _ _ _ _ _ _s baked on top of a pizza are called its t_ _ _ _ _s.

5. The t_ _ _ _ _ _s of the crust is a s_ _ _ _e of local pride.

# Dialog   *Ordering a Pizza by Phone*

会話を聞いた後で＿＿＿に英語を入れてください。

Clerk:　(Ring, ring, ring!) Dominic's Pizza House. May I help you?

Carlos: Yes, I'd like two large pizzas delivered to my apartment.

Clerk: Sure. Would you like New York flatbread or Chicago deep-pan (1)_____?

Carlos: One of each, please. What are the choices for toppings?

Clerk: We have pepperoni, plus nine other meats and vegetables. We can give you "The Works," that's with all the (2)_____ for 9 bucks each. We can deliver them in 15 minutes.

Carlos: Great! Please deliver them to 126 Grand Avenue, apartment 302. My name is Carlos.

Clerk: Thanks, Carlos. Please have exactly $18 ready. The delivery person doesn't carry any (3)_____.

Carlos: No problem. We'll be waiting. Bye.

**Notes** buck 1ドル

## 🎧 Dialog Comprehension

設問に対して適切な解答を選んでください。

1. What is the name of the pizza shop?   ( )
   - a. Chicago's
   - b. New York's
   - c. Clerk's
   - d. Dominic's

2. How many pizzas does Carlos want?   ( )
   - a. Nine
   - b. Two
   - c. 126
   - d. 18

3. Where does he want them delivered?   ( )
   - a. His apartment
   - b. Chicago
   - c. Pizza House
   - d. Bucks

4. What kind of pizzas does he order?   ( )
   - a. Nine kinds
   - b. Vegetables
   - c. The Works
   - d. New York

5. How much will the pizzas cost altogether?   ( )
   - a. $80
   - b. $18
   - c. $126
   - d. Change

# Grammar

**疑問副詞**
when, where, why, how などを疑問副詞といいます。

❶ When は「時」を示します。
**When does the movie start?**
映画はいつ始まりますか。

❷ Where は「場所」を示します。
**Where did you find her?**
彼女をどこで見つけたのですか。

❸ Why は「理由」を示します。
**Why did you go there?**
どうしてそこへ行ったのですか。
この場合、通常 because で答えます。
**Because the entrance fee was free.** 入場料が無料だったからです。

❹ how は「方法・手段・状態」を示します。
**How did you go there?**
どのようにしてそこへ行ったのですか。

次の 1〜3 を英語で書いてください。

1. いつここに着きましたか。私は昨日ここに着きました。(When, arrive)

2. どこに行くのですか。コンビニに行くところです。
   (Where, a convenience store)

3. どうして学校に遅れたのですか。バスに乗り遅れたのです。
   (Why, late for, missed)

### T.G.I.F.

週末をいっぱい楽しんだ人にとって、月曜日は苦痛の始まりです。再び、一週間働かなくてはならないからです。これを Blue Monday と呼び、逆に週末を迎える時は T.G.I.F.（Thank God, it's Friday!）「神様ありがとう、週末です」と喜びを表します。

# Chapter 11
# Holidays in the United States

民族色豊かなアメリカの休日

ニューヨークで大規模に開催される St. Patrick's Day はもともとはアイルランド人のお祭りですが、今では民族や文化的背景を越えて多くの人が祝います。

## Vocabulary

1〜5 と a〜e で、双方の意味が似ているものを結び付けてください。

1. Thanksgiving　　　　a. 民族の
2. government　　　　 b. 感謝祭
3. national holiday　　　c. 政府
4. celebrate　　　　　　d. 祝日
5. ethnic　　　　　　　e. 祝う

# Reading

　The word holiday comes from religious festivals called holy days. But now most holidays in the United States simply mean a day off from work or school to remember some famous person or event. All government offices and most schools and businesses close for the ten yearly national holidays. The most well-known of them internationally are Thanksgiving, Christmas, and New Year's Day.

　America's Independence Day, the Fourth of July, is celebrated all across the United States with parades, fairs and special events, and fireworks in the evening just after sunset. Small towns especially try to outdo their neighbors in making their Fourth of July fireworks as spectacular as their budgets allow.

　However, there are also religious holidays that are widely celebrated, like Easter for Christians, Hanukkah for Jews, and Ramadan for Muslims. There are also holidays for certain ethnic groups. Saint Patrick's Day is a holiday in cities with large Irish populations, as is Martin Luther King Day in cities with many African-Americans. Cinco de Mayo, meaning 5 May, is increasingly being celebrated among Hispanic Americans.

　On such local holidays, you may find local schools or businesses closed. However, federal or national government offices, like post offices, will usually be open.

**Notes**
**Hanukkah** ハヌカー（ユダヤ教の祝祭）　　**Ramadan** ラマダン（イスラム暦の断食月）
**Cinco de Mayo** シンコ・デ・マヨ（メキシコ人の祝日）　　**Hispanic American** 中南米系アメリカ人

*Chapter 11* Holidays in the United States

# Reading Comprehension

英文の内容が適切なら（　）内にT（True）を、そうでない場合はF（False）を入れてください。

1. Holidays used to be called holy days. （　）
2. Independence Day is the First of July. （　）
3. Easter is a religious holiday for Christians. （　）
4. St. Patrick's Day is celebrated mostly among Japanese. （　）
5. Post offices will usually be open on local holidays. （　）

# Word Sense

次の英文を完成してください。

1. Easter is a r_ _ _ _ _ _s festival for C_ _ _ _ _ _ _ _s.
2. G_ _ _ _ _ _ _ _t offices are closed on T_ _ _ _ _ _ _ _ _g.
3. Many, but not all, b_ _ _ _ _ _ _ _s close for n_ _ _ _ _l holidays.
4. Cities with many I_ _ _h-Americans c_ _ _ _ _ _ _e St. Patrick's Day.
5. Some schools c_ _ _e for local h_ _ _ _ _ _s.

# Dialog  *At the St. Patrick's Day Party*    23

会話を聞いた後で＿＿＿に英語を入れてください。

Mariko: Carlos, what are you doing at a St. Patrick's Day party? You're certainly not Irish.

Carlos: And neither are you. But I do like your green dress. How do you like my (1)_____ jacket?

Mariko: It looks great on you, Carlos. But I really don't know why we have to wear green to this party.

Carlos: Green is the national color of Ireland. So, at some (2)_____ parties even the beer is green.

Mariko: And who is St. Patrick anyway and why are we celebrating his day?

Carlos: St. Patrick brought Christianity to Ireland and it became an important part of Irish culture, just like the singing and dancing we're seeing here now.

Mariko: Is it okay for us to join the dancing even though we're not Irish?

Carlos: Mariko, the Irish say that on St. Paddy's (3)_____ everyone is Irish. So, let's dance like we're Irish.

## Dialog Comprehension

設問に対して適切な解答を選んでください。

1. What color is Mariko's dress?  ( )
   a. It's green.           b. He's green.
   c. She's green.          d. They're green.

2. How does Carlos' jacket look on him?  ( )
   a. Green                 b. Like a dress
   c. Great                 d. Like Mariko

3. Why do people wear green on St. Patrick's Day?  ( )
   a. It looks good.                    b. It's Ireland's national color.
   c. It goes well with vegetables.     d. It's America's national color.

4. Who brought Christianity to Ireland?  ( )
   a. The Irish             b. Mariko
   c. Carlos                d. St. Patrick

5. How will Carlos and Mariko dance at the party?  ( )
   a. Like they're Irish    b. Like at a disco
   c. Romantically          d. As if they were friends

# Grammar

**数量を示す形容詞（many・much）**
many と much は数量を示す形容詞です。

❶ many は数えられる名詞の複数形に付けます。
Are there many parks in this city?
この町には多くの公園がありますか。

❷ much は数えられない名詞の複数形に付けます。
Don't eat too much meat.
肉を食べ過ぎないように。

❸ a lot of, lots of, などは many, much に代わる語です。
You have a lot of toys.
君はたくさんのおもちゃを持っている。

次の 1〜3 を英語で書いてください。

1. 彼はこの町に多くの友達を持っていません。（many）

   _____

2. 食べ物はあまり残っていませんね。（There isn't, much, left, is there?）

   _____

3. あなたはこの件で選択の余地がたくさんあるだろうか。（much choice）

   _____

### St. Patrick's Day

ニューヨークではアイルランド人だけでなく多くの人が St. Patrick's Day を祝います。アイルランドを象徴する緑を表すため，緑の服を着，緑のビールを飲み，緑のベーコンを食べる人もいます。この日だけはアイルランド人になって祝ってみるのも楽しいものです。

# Weather in the United States

## さまざまな天候

アメリカは北と南では天候がずいぶん異なります。寒いアラスカ、一年中暖かいフロリダ、砂漠地帯もあります。気候が異なれば人々の生活も異なります。

## Vocabulary

1〜5とa〜eで、双方の意味が似ているものを結び付けてください。

1. climate
2. plain
3. desert
4. temperature
5. tornado

a. 気温
b. 竜巻
c. 気候
d. 平原
e. 砂漠

# Reading

　The United States has many different climates. Hawaii and Florida are warm and Alaska cold all year round. The northern states have cold winters and cool summers, while the southern states have mild winters and hot summers. The United States has long seacoasts, huge mountains, lakes, plains, and deserts. These all cause important changes in its weather. Washington's Mount Rainier has some of the most snow, the Midwest the worst tornados, and California's Death Valley some of the hottest temperatures on Earth.

　However, whatever the weather may be like in an area, the local people find ways of dealing with the bad and enjoying the good. While skaters are playing ice-hockey on the frozen Great Lakes in winter, swimmers are basking in the sun on Florida's beaches. While skiers are enjoying the last of the spring's snows at Aspen in Colorado, surfers are hitting the waves at Malibu in California. It is said that there is no such thing as bad weather, only bad clothes.

　You can experience four distinct seasons in the north or a blending of seasons in the south. No matter what weather you enjoy or need for sports or your health, you can find it somewhere in the United States.

### Notes
**Mount Rainier** レーニア山　　**bask** 日光浴をする　　**Great Lakes** 五大湖　　**no such thing as bad weather, only bad clothes** 悪天候なんてものはない、悪いのはその服装なのさ

# Reading Comprehension

英文の内容が適切なら（　）内にT（True）を、そうでない場合はF（False）を入れてください。

1. Weather is the same all over the United States.　　　　（　）
2. Florida is cold all year round.　　　　（　）
3. Mountains and deserts cause some changes in weather.　　　　（　）
4. Some of the Great Lakes freeze in winter.　　　　（　）
5. The northern United States has only one season.　　　　（　）

# Word Sense

次の英文を完成してください。

1. Florida's c_ _ _ _ _e is very d_ _ _ _ _ _ _t from Alaska's.
2. The United States has long seacoasts, huge m_ _ _ _ _ _ _s and wide p_ _ _ _s.
3. Its lakes and d_ _ _ _s cause changes in its w_ _ _ _ _r.
4. Death V_ _ _ _y is famous for its very hot t_ _ _ _ _ _ _ _ _ _s.
5. In the M_ _ _ _ _t of the United States, people must always be ready for t_ _ _ _ _ _s.

# Dialog  *Spring Break*

会話を聞いた後で____に英語を入れてください。

Carlos:　Mariko, tomorrow is the start of spring break from mid-March to mid-April. What are your plans?

Mariko: I'm tired of Boston's cold winter and all the snow. I'm off to (1)_____ for lots of sun and swimming.

Carlos: Is Florida warm enough for swimming in March?

Mariko: Sure, you can swim there almost all year round. How about your (2)_____?

Carlos: The snow here in New England is gone now that spring has come. But I want to find some more.

Mariko: So, where are you off to? Except Alaska, there's not much snow left anywhere.

Carlos: You forgot the mountains of Colorado. I can ski there right through the (3)_____.

Mariko: That sounds exciting. Let's give each other a report when we come back.

## Dialog Comprehension

設問に対して適切な解答を選んでください。

1. What starts tomorrow? ( )
   a. Lunch          b. Skiing
   c. Spring break   d. April

2. What does Mariko want to do during spring break? ( )
   a. Ski    b. Swim
   c. Shop   d. Study

3. Which place is warm enough for swimming in March? ( )
   a. New England   b. Boston
   c. New York      d. Florida

4. Besides Alaska, where can Carlos find snow in the spring? ( )
   a. Colorado   b. Malibu
   c. Florida    d. Okinawa

5. How long can Carlos ski there? ( )
   a. Through the year    b. Through the break
   c. Through the night   d. During the summer

# Grammar

**the の使い方**
The は一般的に特定の決まったものを指します。

❶ 前に一度出た名詞に付ける場合
I have a car. The car is new.
車を持ってます。それは新車です。

❷ 周囲の状況で何を指しているかが分かっているような場合
Please close the window. It is cold here.
窓を閉めてください。ここは寒いです。

❸ 名詞に形容詞の働きをするものが付いている場合
Who is the man in the room?
部屋の中にいる男の人は誰ですか。

❹ ただ一つしかないものに付ける場合
the sun, the equator（赤道）, the east, the right, など

次の 1〜3 を英語で書いてください。

1. ジョンと幸子は同じ日に生まれました。（were born）

2. 塩を取ってください。（would, pass me, salt）

3. 公園でその少年を見ました。（saw）

 **Signing a cast**

サッカーなどで脚を折ったとき、病院でギプスをつけて安静にします。友人たちがお見舞いに来ると、ギプスに「名前」や「メッセージ」を書き残します。時には、「また、激しくサッカーをやろうぜ！」などというものもあります。これを signing a cast といいます。

# Chapter 13

# Complaining

## 文句を言ってみたい時もあります

外国生活では、文句を言いたくなることがたまにあります。そんなときは、黙っていないでしっかりと自分の立場を主張することです。英語で自らの意思を明確に表すことは難しいですが、英語の練習と思いやってみてください。

## Vocabulary

1〜5 と a〜e で、双方の意味が似ているものを結び付けてください。

1. treat
2. wrong somebody
3. intentionally
4. apology
5. resolve

a. 意図的に
b. 謝罪
c. 解決する
d. 扱う
e. 誰かに不当な扱いをする

# Reading

Nobody likes to complain, to tell others that you have been treated badly or unfairly. But when the computer you just bought stops running the next day, or the restaurant waiter serves you cold soup, or the shop clerk gives you the wrong change, you should not be shy about saying something.

Complain first to the person who wronged you. Usually problems happen by mistake, not intentionally. Normally the computer or soup will be quickly replaced or the correct change given with an apology.

But if the problem is caused by the clerk or waiter's carelessness, or if that person cannot or will not help you, ask to see the boss. Usually that simple request is enough to force waiters or clerks to take care of your problem. Most workers would rather not have their superior know that they have given a customer bad service.

Most companies follow the rule that customers are always right, unless they are clearly wrong. So, managers and supervisors will usually do their best to please their customers. Businesses generally make their money on customers who are pleased with the company's products or services, tell others about their satisfaction, and return to do more business. So, it is good business practice to listen to and resolve a customer's complaints.

### Notes

**change** お釣り　　most workers would rather not have their superior know~
ほとんどの従業員は、上司が~に気付くことを嫌がります。

*Chapter 13* Complaining

# Reading Comprehension

英文の内容が適切なら（　）内に T（True）を、そうでない場合は F（False）を入れてください。

1. Most people enjoy complaining.  (  )

2. Complain first to the person who made the mistake.  (  )

3. Normally a mistake will be corrected and an apology given.  (  )

4. Never ask to see the boss.  (  )

5. It is good business to take care of customer complaints.  (  )

# Word Sense

次の英文を完成してください。

1. Nobody likes to c_ _ _ _ _ _n to o_ _ _ _s.

2. The boss t_ _ _ _ _d his workers u_ _ _ _ _ _y.

3. You should talk f_ _ _t to the person who w_ _ _ _ _d you.

4. The w_ _ _ _r gave me an a_ _ _ _ _y for spilling my coffee.

5. The c_ _ _k gave the wrong change i_ _ _ _ _ _ _ _ _ _ _y to make extra money.

# Dialog  *At the Restaurant*

会話を聞いた後で____に英語を入れてください。

Mariko: Waiter! I ordered a steak dinner over 30 minutes ago and it still hasn't come.

Waiter: Sorry, miss, but your (1)_____ went on break. Please give me a second and I'll check the kitchen. ... Here's your steak, miss.

Mariko: But it's cold. I came here for a nice hot (2)_____ dinner.

Waiter: I'm sorry, miss. I'll ask the cook to warm it up for you.

Mariko: If you expect me to pay for warmed-over steak, you're badly mistaken. I'd like to speak to your boss.

Waiter: If you don't mind waiting, I'll bring you a free drink and have the cook make you a fresh dinner.

Mariko: In that case, I'm hungry, but in no (3)_____. So, I guess I can wait.

Waiter: Thank you for your understanding, miss. I'll tell the boss what happened so it won't happen again.

## Dialog Comprehension

設問に対して適切な解答を選んでください。

1. What did Mariko order?  ( )
   a. Lunch
   b. A cold dinner
   c. A steak
   d. Thirty minutes

2. Why didn't her waiter bring her dinner on time?  ( )
   a. He was on break.
   b. He was the boss.
   c. She was in a hurry.
   d. He was the cook.

3. Why wouldn't she pay for the steak she got?  ( )
   a. She was hot.
   b. It was cold.
   c. He was not her waiter.
   d. It was a steak.

4. While she is waiting for the fresh dinner, what will the waiter give her?  ( )
   a. More time
   b. A long wait
   c. A cold steak
   d. A free drink

5. Who will the waiter tell about what happened?  ( )
   a. The boss
   b. The cook
   c. Mariko
   d. The waiter

# Grammar

**冠詞の省略**
次のような場合は冠詞を省略します。

❶ 家族内の人を指し示すとき
Mother isn't at home now.
母は今、家にいません。

❷ 場所や建物が本来そこで行う動作や機能を示す場合
I go to bed at eleven.
11時に寝ます。
School begins at eight.
学校は8時に始まります。

❸ 季節・月・曜日・休日などの名前
I like spring better than other seasons.
ほかの季節より春が好きです。

❹ 慣用句などの表現
by bus（バスで）　after school（放課後）　at night（夜に）

次の1〜3を英語で書いてください。

1. あなたは大学に4年間行かなければなりません。(have to go, for)

   _____

2. 2014年の夏に、私はニューヨークに行きました。(New York, in)

   _____

3. 彼はクリスマスの前にはここにいるでしょう。(will be here, before, Christmas)

   _____

 **Tipping**

アメリカのタクシーではTipが要ります。通常、運賃の15〜20％ぐらいです。でも、運転手の態度がひどいときは、チップを払う必要はありません。運転手に料金を払う時、アメリカ人はタクシーを降りてから、助手席の窓越しに払う人がいます。

# Chapter 14 Farmers' Markets

ファーマーズマーケット

ファーマーズマーケットでは農家の人が自分で作った野菜、果物、チーズ、クッキー、ハム、ジャムなどさまざまなものを売っています。大きなマーケットは野球場ぐらいあります。地元の人や観光客でいっぱいです。

## Vocabulary

1～5 と a～e で、双方の意味が似ているものを結び付けてください。

1. farmers' markets
2. spring up
3. consumer
4. the town square
5. handiwork

a. 手芸品
b. ファーマーズマーケット
c. 現れる
d. 消費者
e. 町の広場

# Reading

From late spring to early fall, farmers' markets spring up in small towns, even in some large cities, across the United States. These markets allow farmers to sell their fruits, vegetables, and sometimes homemade cheese, sausages, bread, and cakes directly to the consumers, the people who will eat them.

In small towns, these markets are often run by the local government in the town square or park on Saturday mornings. The local farmers pay a small fee to set up their tables on the ground and sell their produce at far below store prices. Their customers are happy with the low prices, the freshness of the food, and the joy of knowing the farmers who produced it.

The hours and days of farmers' markets in cities vary and the prices are a bit higher, but the food is equally fresh. Craftspeople and artists are also allowed to sell their handiwork at the markets.

Local supermarkets are surprisingly happy to have the markets nearby. They find that the markets draw customers to the area for vegetables, but they then go to the supermarkets to buy non-local foods and other products.

There are over 8,000 farmers' markets listed in the United States, with over 120 of them in New York City.

**Notes**
**be often run by** たいていは〜によって運営される　　**produce** 農産物（野菜や果物）
**craftspeople** 工芸品などの職人

# Reading Comprehension

英文の内容が適切なら（　）内に T（True）を、そうでない場合は F（False）を入れてください。

1. Farmers' markets are usually open only in winter. （　）
2. Farmers can sell their produce directly to consumers. （　）
3. Customers are happy with the freshness of the food. （　）
4. Supermarkets are angry about having a farmers' market nearby. （　）
5. There are over 8,000 farmers' markets listed in the United States. （　）

# Word Sense

次の英文を完成してください。

1. Farmers sell their v_____s directly to their c_____s.
2. Customers enjoy k_____g the farmers who p_____e the food they buy.
3. Craftspeople are also a_____d to sell their h_____k.
4. The days of f_____s' markets v__y in cities.
5. Customers go to a s_____t to buy non-local f__d.

# Dialog  *The Farmers' Market*

会話を聞いた後で____に英語を入れてください。

Mariko: Carlos, have you heard of the farmers' market in Copley Square on Tuesdays?

Carlos: Sure, it's on (1)_____, too. I go at lunch-time twice a week to buy fresh vegetables.

Mariko: How fresh are the vegetables and how about the prices?

Carlos: The (2)_____ are really cheap and the farmers pick their stuff that very morning.

Mariko: I guess food can't get fresher than that. Do they sell anything else?

Carlos: Of course. They also sell (3)_____ cheese and really delicious cakes and pies.

Mariko: You'd better watch your waist, Carlos, eating all those delicious fattening foods.

Carlos: No problem. I eat carefully and trust the farmers to sell only healthy foods.

**Notes** fattening food 太るもとになる食品

## Dialog Comprehension

設問に対して適切な解答を選んでください。

1. When does Carlos go to the market?      ( )
   a. At lunch-time          b. In winter
   c. In early spring        d. At New Years

2. How often does Carlos go to the farmers' market?    ( )
   a. Daily                  b. On Saturdays
   c. Once a year            d. Twice a week

3. How are the prices at the market?     ( )
   a. Very high              b. Cheap
   c. The same as at stores  d. Normal

4. What do the farmers sell besides fruits and vegetables?    ( )
   a. Cakes                  b. Cars
   c. Supermarkets           d. Consumers

5. Why won't Carlos get fat?     ( )
   a. He eats carefully.         b. Mariko loves cake.
   c. Cake is not fattening.     d. The vegetables are fresh.

# Grammar

**it のさまざまな使い方。**
英語には it を仮主語として使う場合があります。

❶ 「時間・距離」を表す it
It is twelve now. Let's have lunch.
12 時だから、昼食にしよう。
How far is it to your school?
学校までどれくらいの距離ですか。

❷ 「天候・寒暖」を表す it
It looks like rain.
雨になりそうだ。
It was very cold that morning.
その朝はとても寒かった。

❸ 「明暗・季節」を表す it
It gets bright early at this time of year.
一年のこの頃は明るくなるのが早いです。

次の 1～3 を英語で書いてください。

1. 何時ですか。(What time)

   _____

2. 夏には蒸し暑くなります。(It gets, humid, in)

   _____

3. 駅まで 2 マイルです。(It is, miles, to)

   _____

 The farmers' market

土・日の朝にファーマーズマーケットが開かれます。新鮮な野菜や果物など、農家の人が自分で作ったものを売っています。どれもおいしそうで買い物袋は瞬く間にいっぱいになります。

# Chapter 15

# Volunteering

## 文化を学ぶためにボランティア体験

アメリカ人を知るために、そして英語を学ぶために、アメリカ社会の基盤を担っているボランティアに参加してみるのもよいかもしれません。

## Vocabulary

1〜5 と a〜e で、双方の意味が似ているものを結び付けてください。

1. overlooked way
2. for a cause
3. patient
4. lead activities
5. reward

a. 活動の手助けをする
b. 見返り
c. 見落されている方法
d. ある目的のために
e. 患者

# Reading

An often overlooked way of making friends and improving language skills is by volunteering. Whether long-term visitors to the U.S. can work or not depends on their type of visa. However, anyone can volunteer, work without pay for a cause.

There are plenty of opportunities waiting for those who are willing to do it. Hospitals and senior citizen or old folks homes often need people just to talk to their patients or perhaps lead activities. No special skills are required, just a friendly face and a willingness to talk and listen.

Schools also need teaching assistants to give extra help in math or other subjects, especially to very young students. Small towns and villages often ask for volunteers to plant flowers, clean the parks, watch over children on the playgrounds, or act as lifeguards at the pools. In many small towns, both the firefighters and ambulance drivers are volunteers. Such work requires special training and it is given for free to volunteers.

These are only a few of the opportunities to volunteer in a community. There is no pay, but the rewards are great. The volunteers have the joy of helping people in need, learning new skills, and becoming part of their community.

**Notes**
work without pay for a cause ある目的のために無報酬で働く　　become part of their community 地域社会の一員となる

Chapter 15 Volunteering

# Reading Comprehension

英文の内容が適切なら（　）内に T（True）を、そうでない場合は F（False）を入れてください。

1. Volunteering is a way of making friends. （　）
2. Anyone can get a well-paid job in the United States. （　）
3. Volunteers can make a lot of money in small towns. （　）
4. Teacher assistants help students with math and other subjects. （　）
5. Training for volunteer firefighters is free. （　）

# Word Sense

次の英文を完成してください。

1. Volunteering is an o_ _ _ _ _ _ _ _d way of making f_ _ _ _s.
2. Senior c_ _ _ _ _n homes need volunteers just to talk to their p_ _ _ _ _ _s.
3. Teacher a_ _ _ _ _ _ _ _s give extra help to students in some s_ _ _ _ _ _s.
4. Ambulance d_ _ _ _ _s need special t_ _ _ _ _ _g.
5. Volunteers b_ _ _ _e part of t_ _ _r community.

# Dialog   *The Volunteer*    31

会話を聞いた後で＿＿＿に英語を入れてください。

Mariko: Carlos, how's your new volunteer job at the hospital going?

Carlos: Great! I'm helping kids who'll be in the (1)_____ a long time keep up with their school work.

Mariko: Now that's a laugh! You, teaching American kids English?

Carlos: Not English, but other subjects, like (2)_____ or science where my English is good enough.

Mariko: I wouldn't think that kids in a hospital would feel much like studying.

Carlos: They don't, but they're bored and lonely. So, I try to make the lessons fun.

Mariko: That's a lot of work for no pay. Why do you (3)_____ to do it?

Carlos: Well, I love working with kids and it's a great chance for me to practice my English.

## Dialog Comprehension

設問に対して適切な解答を選んでください。

1. Where is Carlos volunteering?  ( )
   - a. At a school
   - b. At a hospital
   - c. In a classroom
   - d. At an old folks home

2. Who is he teaching?  ( )
   - a. Kids
   - b. Doctors
   - c. Nurses
   - d. Teachers

3. What does he teach them?  ( )
   - a. English
   - b. Driving
   - c. American history
   - d. Science

4. How does Carlos interest the children in studying?  ( )
   - a. He is lonely.
   - b. They are boring.
   - c. He makes lessons fun.
   - d. They like Mariko.

5. Why does Carlos volunteer?  ( )
   - a. To teach English
   - b. To practice English
   - c. Because he's bored
   - d. To be a doctor

# Grammar

**再帰代名詞**
~self (~selves) の形を再帰代名詞といいます。

❶ 前置詞（of, for, by など）の目的語となるもの。
Please take good care of yourself.
どうぞお大事に。
Look up the word in the dictionary by yourself.
自分自身で、その単語を辞書で調べなさい。
How did she catch him by herself?
彼女はどのようにして一人で彼を捕まえたのですか。

❷ 慣用的な表現。
He applied himself to learning French.
彼はフランス語の勉強に専念した。
Kate found herself in front of the shop.
ケイトは気づいたら店の前に立っていた。

次の1〜3を英語で書いてください。

1. 彼女は自分自身を知るべきだ。（should, herself）

2. 歴史は繰り返すというのは本当だ。（It is true that, repeats, itself）

3. ケーキを自由に食べてください。（Please help yourself, to）

**Soup kitchen**

ホームレスの人たちに食事を提供する施設を soup kitchen（スープ・キッチン）と呼びます。教会関係者やボランティアの人たちが食事や日用品を配ります。アメリカの社会でも貧困層と富裕層との格差問題は深刻です。

# Chapter 16

# College Towns

## 活気あふれる大学町

college town は世界各国出身の学生でにぎわっています。各国の料理を提供する色々なレストランもあります。大学の授業など、地元住民に無料で提供されているところもあります。

## Vocabulary

1～5 と a～e で、双方の意味が似ているものを結び付けてください。

1. be considered
2. a small fee
3. local resident
4. provide
5. ghost towns

a. 地元住民
b. 提供する
c. ゴーストタウン（人がいなくなった町）
d. ～とみなされる
e. わずかな料金

# Reading

A "college town" may well be a village with a small junior college or big city with many universities. But if students make up a large part of the population and play a major role in the economy and culture of the community, it is considered a college town.

Generally, college towns are fun and interesting places to live, work, or study. Many of the school facilities, such as libraries, pools, gyms, or even medical centers are open to the public for a small fee. Local residents can also attend classes, and some lectures are even free. Of course, everyone is welcome at school sports and many other social events.

The schools provide jobs for the community, and their students are important customers for local businesses. Because of the large number of students in such communities, the kinds of shops and the goods they sell are aimed at young people who come not only from across America but from all over the world. So, the culture of a college town is usually international, especially in its food, music, and fashion. Restaurants serve and supermarkets sell food from every country in the world.

But during vacation times, when most students return home, many college towns become ghost towns, places with very few people and lots of empty shops.

**Notes**
**be open to the public** 一般の人に開放されている

# Reading Comprehension

英文の内容が適切なら（　）内にT（True）を、そうでない場合はF（False）を入れてください。

1. A "college town" may be a big city.   (   )

2. College towns are usually quite boring.   (   )

3. Students do not buy much from local businesses.   (   )

4. College towns often have international restaurants.   (   )

5. During summer vacation, college towns are always full of people.   (   )

# Word Sense

次の英文を完成してください。

1. Students p_ _y a major r_ _e in the economy.

2. Many school f_ _ _ _ _ _ _ _s are open to the p_ _ _ _c.

3. Schools p_ _ _ _ _e jobs for people in the c_ _ _ _ _ _ _y.

4. College t_ _ _s have an i_ _ _ _ _ _ _ _ _ _ _ _l culture.

5. The g_ _ _t town was full of e_ _ _y shops.

# Dialog   *The College Town*

会話を聞いた後で____に英語を入れてください。

Mariko: Carlos, how did you spend your weekend?

**Chapter 16** *College Towns*

Carlos: I took in a free violin concert at Berklee College of Music. How about you?

Mariko: I saw *Hamlet* on (1)_____ night in Boston Common. It was free, too.

Carlos: In the park? Who put on the play and where did you sit?

Mariko: It was an amateur theater club from Harvard. We all just sat on the (2)_____. It was fabulous!

Carlos: It sounds great. That's the joy of a college town like Boston.

Mariko: With all the (3)_____ and universities here, there's always something going on.

Carlos: And mostly free. Speaking of money, I'm going out for Mexican. If you don't mind Dutch treat, you can join me.

**Notes** Dutch treat 割り勘

## Dialog Comprehension

設問に対して適切な解答を選んでください。

1. How did Carlos spend his weekend?   (   )
   a. He played music.         b. He studied at school.
   c. He went to a concert.    d. He took a class at Berkely.

2. How much did it cost?   (   )
   a. It was free.             b. It was cheap.
   c. It was expensive.        d. There was a large fee.

3. What play did Mariko see?   (   )
   a. Boston                   b. Park
   c. Common                   d. *Hamlet*

4. Who put on the play?   (   )
   a. The grass                b. A theater club
   c. Mariko                   d. Carlos

5. What kind of food will Carlos have tonight?   (   )
   a. American                 b. Dutch
   c. Mexican                  d. Boston

# Grammar

**副詞**
副詞は動詞・形容詞・副詞・文などを修飾します。

❶ 動詞を修飾する副詞
Read the letter carefully.
手紙を注意深く読んでください。
（この場合 carefully は、read という動詞を修飾しています）

❷ 形容詞を修飾する副詞
It was a very fine morning.
とても素晴らしい朝でした。
（この場合 very は、fine という形容詞を修飾しています）

❸ 副詞を修飾する副詞
He spoke terribly slowly.
彼はとてもゆっくり話しました。
（この場合 terribly は、slowly という副詞を修飾しています）

❹ 文全体を修飾する副詞
Probably the news is true.
おそらくそのニュースは事実だろう。
（この場合 probably は、文全体を修飾しています）

次の1～3を英語で書いてください。

1. リリーは上手に踊りました。(Lily, well)

2. テストは簡単でした。(The test, easy)

3. そんなに早く走らないで。(Don't run, so)

**SAT**

アメリカでは大学入試がありません。SAT（Scholastic Assessment Test）大学進学適性試験や高校の成績、推薦状、時には面接などで入学が決まります。入学後は厳しい勉学が待っていて卒業は難しいです。日本とは正反対です。

# Chapter 17

# American History

アメリカの歴史

価値観の異なるさまざまな人たちが共に生きるために、アメリカでは「自由と平等」の信念が必要です。

## Vocabulary

1〜5 と a〜e で、双方の意味が似ているものを結び付けてください。

1. revolution
2. government
3. independent
4. limit
5. assembly

a. 政府
b. 独立した
c. 限界
d. 集会
e. 革命

# Reading

The American Revolution made the United States independent from Britain. The Civil War gave the United States government the power to hold the country together. World Wars I and II made it a world power. But its wars in Korea, Vietnam, Iraq, and Afghanistan showed the limits of that power.

Unlike the people of most countries, the people of the United States are held together, not by blood, but by the idea that they make their own government and its rules. So, Americans are all both equal and free. They have given themselves the right to freedom of speech, religion, assembly, and many other important rights. As Abraham Lincoln said, the American government is "of the people, by the people, and for the people."

However, as Americans move further from their revolution, they face the danger of forgetting its causes and the value of the ideals of democracy it has given them. Each generation must learn those ideals and teach them in turn to America's new immigrants. For, unless the ideals of democracy are accepted and work to the benefit of all, the United States cannot continue to prosper.

For over two hundred years now, the people of the United States have been democratically working to make sure their ideals are preserved and their rights are shared equally. That work will never end.

**Notes**

the American Revolution アメリカ独立戦争 (1775-83)　　the Civil War 南北戦争 (1861-65)

Chapter 17 American History

# Reading Comprehension

英文の内容が適切なら（　）内に T（True）を、そうでない場合は F（False）を入れてください。

1. The United States became independent from Britain.  (　)

2. The Civil War made the United States a world power.  (　)

3. The people of the United States are held together by ties of blood.  (　)

4. Americans have freedom of speech.  (　)

5. The United States is less than two-hundred-years old.  (　)

# Word Sense

次の英文を完成してください。

1. The American R_ _ _ _ _ _ _ _n made the U_ _ _ _d States a new country.

2. The United States became i_ _ _ _ _ _ _ _ _t from B_ _ _ _ _n.

3. Freedom of a_ _ _ _ _ _y, being able to get together to talk, is an i_ _ _ _ _ _ _t right.

4. The latest wars of the United States have shown the l_ _ _ _s of its p_ _ _r in the world.

5. Every g_ _ _ _ _ _ _ _t tries to hold its country t_ _ _ _ _ _r.

# Dialog  *The Civil War (1861-1865)*

会話を聞いた後で____に英語を入れてください。

Mariko: How was your history lesson on the Civil War today with Professor Jones?

Carlos: She's a great teacher, but I still don't (1)_____ why Americans had to fight a war with each other.

Mariko: In 1861, the southern states broke away from the United States to make their own country.

Carlos: Was that because the South used slaves and the North didn't?

Mariko: Yes, but the South's culture was also different from the (2)_____. So, Southerners wanted to be independent.

Carlos: Why couldn't President Abraham Lincoln let them go their own way?

Mariko: Lincoln believed that if the country fell apart, the American Revolution would lose its meaning.

Carlos: So, that's why he was willing to fight a (3)_____ war. Thanks.

## Dialog Comprehension

設問に対して適切な解答を選んでください。

1. What was Carlos' history lesson about?  ( )
   a. Japan
   b. Teachers
   c. Jones
   d. The Civil War

2. What did the South use that the North did not?  ( )
   a. Slaves
   b. Wars
   c. History
   d. Food

3. When did the South break away from the United States?  ( )
   a. Before independence
   b. Because of slavery
   c. Before 1860
   d. In 1861

4. Why did Southerners want to be independent?  ( )
   a. They had slaves.
   b. They lost their meaning.
   c. Their culture was different.
   d. Lincoln would not let them.

5. Who was willing to fight a civil war to keep the United States together?  ( )
   a. Southerners
   b. Jones
   c. Lincoln
   d. The revolution

# Grammar

**命令文**
命令文は主語を省略し、動詞の原型で文を始めます。

❶ be 動詞の原型を使う命令文
Be kind to others.　他人に親切にしなさい。
(be を使うことに注意してください)

❷ 「〜をしましょう」と相手を誘う文
Let's play tennis.　さあ、テニスをしましょう。

❸ be 動詞の否定の命令文
Don't be late for the class.　授業に遅れないでください。
be 動詞の前に don't を付けます。

次の 1〜3 を英語で書いてください。

1. パスポートを見せてください。(Please, show, passport)

2. 急ぎません。時間をかけてください。(Don't, hurry, Take, time)

3. 英語を学びましょう。(Let's)

 Lincoln

多民族のアメリカでは、国民が一つにならなければなりません。リンカーンの言葉 "The government of the people, by the people, and for the people"(国民のための、国民による、国民の統治)はあまりにも有名な言葉です。1776 年に東部 13 植民地が独立宣言をしてから、現在は 50 州あります。

# Chapter 18

# Native Americans

## アメリカの先住民

1492年、コロンブスは到着地をアジアのインドの一部と信じたので、アメリカにすでに住んでいる人をインディアンと呼んでしまったのです。

## Vocabulary

1～5とa～eで、双方の意味が似ているものを結び付けてください。

1. permanent
2. revolution
3. last
4. harvest
5. be pushed off

a. 収穫
b. 追いやられる
c. 永続的な
d. 改革
e. 続く

# Reading

On 16 September 1620, a ship called *Mayflower* left Plymouth, England, on its way to America with 102 passengers (Pilgrims). They landed at a place we now call Plymouth, Massachusetts, on 16 December the same year. They started the first permanent English settlement in America. By the fall of 1621, only 53 of them were still alive, but they had made friends with the local Indians who taught them how to farm, hunt, and fish in their new home. They celebrated their first harvest, now called Thanksgiving Day, with their Indian friends.

Unfortunately, friendly relations did not last long. As more and more English and other Europeans came to America, the Indians were pushed off their lands and finally into reservations, places where they could continue their traditional way of life as Native Americans.

When the *Mayflower* arrived, there were several million Indians living in what is now the United States. However, diseases brought by the settlers from Europe and frequent wars between the settlers and Indians have cut that number to between three and five million today. About one million Native Americans now live on reservations, mostly in the southwest of the United States.

Although all Native Americans were made citizens in 1924, those who live on reservations also have the right to make local laws and to govern their own reservations.

**Notes**
**Thanksgiving Day** 感謝祭（11月の第4木曜日）　　**reservation** 先住民居留地

# Reading Comprehension

英文の内容が適切なら（　）内に T（True）を、そうでない場合は F（False）を入れてください。

1. The *Mayflower* left England in September 1620.　　　（　）

2. It landed at Plymouth, Massachusetts, the next year.　　　（　）

3. All 102 Pilgrims ate Thanksgiving dinner with the Indians.　　　（　）

4. Native Americans can continue their traditional lifestyle on reservations.　　　（　）

5. Native Americans are not American citizens.　　　（　）

# Word Sense

次の英文を完成してください。

1. The first permanent E_ _ _ _ _h settlement in North America was at P_ _ _ _ _ _h.

2. Native A_ _ _ _ _ _ _s were pushed off their lands and put into r_ _ _ _ _ _ _ _ _s.

3. There were several m_ _ _ _ _n Native Americans in the present United States when the P_ _ _ _ _ _s arrived.

4. Most I_ _ _ _n reservations are in the s_ _ _ _ _ _ _t of the United States.

5. N_ _ _ _e Americans g_ _ _ _n their own reservations.

# Dialog  *Native Americans*   37

会話を聞いた後で____に英語を入れてください。

Mariko: Carlos, my new literature teacher is an Indian!

Carlos: What's so special about that. There are lots of people from India here.

Mariko: No, not an Indian American, but an American (1)_____, a Native American.

Carlos: A Native American? Does he live on a reservation?

Mariko: Not anymore. He was born on a reservation, but now lives and (2)_____ here.

Carlos: That's a shame. If I were an Indian, I'd rather live a traditional lifestyle than work in the city.

Mariko: He says he goes home to the (3)_____ sometimes to hunt and fish with his relatives.

Carlos: Wow! If you introduce me to him, maybe he'll take me along!

## Dialog Comprehension

設問に対して適切な解答を選んでください。

1. Who is Mariko's new literature teacher? ( )
   a. An Indian American
   b. A man from India
   c. A Native American
   d. A woman from a reservation

2. Where was he born? ( )
   a. In a city
   b. On a reservation
   c. In India
   d. Here in town

3. How would Carlos live if he were a Native American? ( )
   a. As a worker
   b. Like Indian Americans
   c. As a teacher
   d. Traditionally

4. Who does Mariko's teacher hunt and fish with? ( )
   a. Carlos
   b. His relatives
   c. Other teachers
   d. Mariko

5. What would Carlos like to do with Mariko's teacher? ( )
   a. Hunt
   b. Work
   c. Party
   d. Teach

# Grammar

**動詞の過去形**
動詞は現在・過去・過去分詞と活用します。

❶ 規則動詞
大部分は {原型 + (e)d} で過去形と過去分詞を作ります。
walk, walked, walked
動詞の語尾が e の場合、d だけを付けます。　use, used, used
動詞の語尾が子音字＋y なら、y を i に変えて ed を付けます。
study, studied, studied
動詞の語尾が短母音＋1つの子音字なら、子音字を重ねて ed を付けます。
stop (stopped) (stopped)

❷ 不規則動詞の4つのパターン
　1) ABC 型　　give, gave, given
　2) ABB 型　　say, said, said
　3) ABA 型　　come, came, come
　4) AAA 型　　cut, cut, cut

次の1〜3を英語で書いてください。

1. 彼は先週、美術館に行きました。（a museum, last week）

   _____

2. メアリーは妹の宿題を手伝いました。（Mary, helped, homework）

   _____

3. 彼女はスープに塩を少し加えました。（added, salt, the soup）

   _____

**Native Americans**

アメリカの先住民 Native Americans（Indian）は日本人と同じモンゴロイド系で宗教や儀式、習慣などに日本人と多くの点で似ているところがあります。太古の昔に日本人とどのような関係があったのでしょうか。興味深い点です。

# The Government of the United States

アメリカの政府

アメリカの連邦議会は上院（各州2名選出・合計100名・6年任期）そして下院は（人口の比率により現在435名を選出・2年任期）から成ります。大統領は国民の直接選挙で選ばれ任期は4年です。

## Vocabulary

1〜5とa〜eで、双方の意味が似ているものを結び付けてください。

1. be appointed by
2. in line with
3. serve
4. federation
5. carry out

a. 〜によって任命される
b. 〜に沿って
c. 任期を務める
d. 連邦
e. 遂行する

# Reading

The government of the United States of America is often called the federal government because it represents the federation or association of its 50 states. It is led by the president, the Congress, and the Supreme Court.

Congress makes the laws of the U.S. and taxes the people to pay for its work. Congress is made up of the Senate and the House of Representatives, simply called the House. Each of the 50 states sends two senators to the Senate. They each serve for six years. Each state also sends representatives to the House, based on its population. They serve for two-year terms. Now there are 435 representatives in it.

The Supreme Court makes sure that the laws made by Congress are in line with the Constitution of the United States, the basic law of the land. Its nine judges are appointed by the president with the agreement of the Senate.

The president's job is to represent the United States in the world, lead the United States military, and carry out the laws that Congress makes. He is elected for a four-year term by winning the votes of a majority of American voters. He cannot serve more than two terms.

The system is supposed to separate power so that neither Congress, nor the Supreme Court, nor the president can hold all the power of government.

**Notes**
the Congress 連邦議会    the Supreme Court 最高裁判所    the Senate 上院
the House of Representatives 下院    the Constitution of the United States アメリカ合衆国憲法

*Chapter 19* *The Government of the United States*

# Reading Comprehension

英文の内容が適切なら（　）内に T（True）を、そうでない場合は F（False）を入れてください。

1. The United States has fifty states. (　)
2. The president makes its laws. (　)
3. Each state sends six senators to Congress. (　)
4. The Supreme Court has nine judges. (　)
5. Congress holds all the power in the government of the United States. (　)

# Word Sense

次の英文を完成してください。

1. Making l_ _s is the job of the C_ _ _ _ _ _s.
2. Each s_ _ _e has two s_ _ _ _ _ _s in the Senate.
3. There are 435 r_ _ _ _ _ _ _ _ _ _ _ _ _s in the H_ _ _e.
4. The C_ _ _ _ _ _ _ _ _ _n is the b_ _ _c law of the United States.
5. The p_ _ _ _ _ _ _t must win a m_ _ _ _ _ _y of the votes.

# Dialog  *Headline News*

会話を聞いた後で____に英語を入れてください。

Mariko: Carlos, did you see the newspaper? Some guy with a gun killed a bunch of kids at a school.

Carlos: Why doesn't the president just take the (1)_____ away from all these crazy people?

Mariko: He can't do that unless Congress gives him the power by passing a law.

Carlos: Then why doesn't Congress pass a (2)_____ saying people can't have guns?

Mariko: The Constitution of the United States lets Americans own guns. Congress and the Supreme Court agree with that.

Carlos: But the president can just send soldiers around to pick up all the guns. How can Congress stop him?

Mariko: Easy. The president's money comes from Congress. Without it he can't even pay the (3)_____.

Carlos: What a strange system! The president in my country can do whatever he wants.

## Dialog Comprehension

設問に対して適切な解答を選んでください。

1. Where did Mariko see the news?　　　( )
   a. On TV　　　　　　　　b. In the newspaper
   c. At a school　　　　　d. In a club

2. What must Congress do to give the president power?　　　( )
   a. Go to school　　　　　b. Talk to him
   c. Use a gun　　　　　　d. Pass a law

3. Why can Americans own guns?　　　( )
   a. Congress buys them.　　　b. The Supreme Court is Congress.
   c. The Constitution lets them.　　d. The president loves guns.

4. Where does the president's money come from?　　　( )
   a. Carlos　　　　　　　　b. Congress
   c. The Supreme Court　　d. The Constitution

5. Without money, who can't he pay?　　　( )
   a. The soldiers　　　　　b. The guns
   c. Congress　　　　　　d. Senators

# Grammar

**関係代名詞**
who, which, that, what などを関係代名詞といいます。

❶ who は「先行詞が人」のときに使います。
Kate is a nurse who helps sick people.
ケイとは病気の人を助ける看護師です。

❷ which は「先行詞がもの」のときに使います。
I bought a book which was written by Tanizaki.
私は谷崎によって書かれた本を買いました。

❸ that は「先行詞が最上級」のときなどに使います。
He is the greatest man that has ever lived in this town.
彼はかつてこの町に住んだ中でもっとも偉大な人です。

❹ what は「先行詞」が含まれているときに使います。
What (The thing that) caused the accident was a broken traffic light.
事故の原因は、壊れた交通信号機でした。

次の1〜3を関係代名詞を使って英語で書いてください。

1. 私は東京に住んでいる友達を知っています。(a friend who lives)

2. 私は忠実な犬を持っています。(have, a dog which, faithful)

3. 彼女は僕が今まで見た中で最も高価な時計をしている。
   (wears, the most expensive, that I have ever seen)

**Little Italy**

ニューヨーク市中心部マンハッタンの Little Italy には、イタリア系の人が多く住んでいます。イタリアンレストランやイタリアの食料品店などもあります。イタリア語も耳にします。イタリアから移民してきた年老いたイタリア人には、イタリアの空気を味わうことができる懐かしい場所なのでしょう。

# Chapter 20
# Washington, District of Columbia (D.C.)

政治の中心ワシントン

首都ワシントンには172カ国・地域の大使館があります。博物館や美術館が並ぶ中心部のナショナルモールには、有名なスミソニアン博物館があります。

## Vocabulary

1〜5 と a〜e で、双方の意味が似ているものを結び付けてください。

1. lively
2. monuments
3. foreign embassies
4. be run by
5. state

a. 州
b. 〜によって運営されている
c. 外国の大使館
d. 記念建造物
e. 活気のある

# Reading

The United States has a state called Washington on its west coast and a city called Washington, D.C., or simply D.C., on its east coast. D.C. is not in any state. It is the political capital of the United States and is run by the Congress of the United States. The people elect their own mayor and other leaders. However, D.C.'s budget and any laws it makes must be approved by Congress, and D.C. has no members in Congress.

D.C. has a little over half a million citizens, but on weekdays the actual number of people in the city doubles to over a million. The main business of D.C. is the government and it employs about 30 percent of the city's population. Because some members of Congress with their staff change every two years and foreign embassies often change their staff, there are always old citizens leaving and new ones coming in.

The next biggest employer is tourism. Every day thousands of tourists come to D.C. to visit the Capitol, the White House, the Supreme Court, and the many museums and monuments in and around the National Mall. Because of all this movement, D.C. is a very lively city, constantly renewing itself, so much so that meeting someone born there may come as a surprise.

## Notes

**Washington, D.C.** 米国の首都で連邦直轄地　　**the Capitol** 連邦議会議事堂　　**the White House** アメリカ大統領官邸　　**the National Mall** ワシントンの中心部にある国立公園

# Reading Comprehension

英文の内容が適切なら（　）内にT（True）を、そうでない場合はF（False）を入れてください。

1. Washington, D.C. is a state. （　）
2. The people of D.C. elect their own leaders. （　）
3. D.C. has several members in Congress. （　）
4. The people in Congress and their staff never change. （　）
5. Washington Mall has many museums surrounding it. （　）

# Word Sense

次の英文を完成してください。

1. W_ _ _ _ _ _ _n, D.C. is the political c_ _ _ _l of the United States.
2. Its l_ _s must be approved by C_ _ _ _ _ _s.
3. The p_ _ _ _ _ _ _n of the city d_ _ _ _s on weekdays.
4. Foreign e_ _ _ _ _ _s often change their s_ _ _f.
5. The population of this l_ _ _ _y city is constantly r_ _ _ _ _ _g itself.

# Dialog  *Washington*

会話を聞いた後で＿＿＿に英語を入れてください。

Mariko: Carlos, how was your conference in Washington?

Carlos: Great, but the city was really impressive with its government buildings and monuments.

Mariko: Did you visit the National Art Gallery and other (1)_____ around the Mall?

Carlos: And the Smithsonian, of course. But even more fun was the nightlife.

Mariko: I've heard that it's easy to make friends in D.C. because there are lots of lonely (2)_____.

Carlos: On top of that, there are open parties everywhere. I went to one at my country's embassy.

Mariko: That must have been fun, to eat food from your home country again.

Carlos: You bet! But, because of demand from the (3)_____, you can eat food from any country in D.C.

**Notes** on top of that それに加えて

## Dialog Comprehension

設問に対して適切な解答を選んでください。

1. What impressed Carlos about D.C.?  ( )
   a. The traffic          b. The monuments
   c. The population       d. The newcomers

2. Where are many of D.C.'s museums?  ( )
   a. Around the Mall      b. At the White House
   c. In Congress          d. Along the river

3. What was more fun for Carlos than the Smithsonian?  ( )
   a. The museums          b. The monuments
   c. The nightlife        d. The government

4. Why is it easy to make friends with new-comers in D.C.?  ( )
   a. They live in D.C.    b. There is food from other countries.
   c. They are staff.      d. They're lonely.

5. Who held the party Carlos went to?  ( )
   a. His good friend      b. Mariko
   c. His embassy          d. The new-comers

# Grammar

**It~to.... の構文**

It~to.... はよく使われる重要な構文です。
It は形式的には主語ですが、意味上は to... の部分が主語になります。
したがって、It は「それは」という意味を持ちません。

❶ It~to.... の構文　to 以下が主語
It is important to think about us.
私たちのことを考えるのは重要です。

❷ It~for....to.... の構文
It is difficult for me to learn English.
英語を勉強するのは私にとって難しいです。

❸ It~of....to.... の構文　to 以下が主語
It was foolish of you to believe her.
彼女を信じるなんて君は愚かだよ。

次の 1～3 を英語で書いてください。

1. その質問に答えるのは簡単でない。（It is not, answer）

   _____

2. 英語を話すのは私にとってやさしい。（It is, for me）

   _____

3. 私を助けてくれるとはニックは親切だ。（It is, kind of, Nick）

   _____

 **Washington, District of Columbia (D.C.)**

首都ワシントンはアメリカの政治の中心です。大統領はホワイトハウスに住んでいます。国防総省の建物は五角形をしているので the Pentagon（ペンタゴン）と呼ばれています。

## TEXT PRODUCTION STAFF

<u>edited by</u>　　　　編集
Eiichi Kanno　　　菅野英一
Kimio Sato　　　　佐藤公雄

<u>English-language editing by</u>　英文校閲
Bill Benfield　　　ビル・ベンフィールド

<u>cover design by</u>　　表紙デザイン
Ruben Frosali　　　ルーベン・フロサリ

## CD PRODUCTION STAFF

<u>recorded by</u>　　　　　　吹き込み者
Rachel Walzer (AmE)　レイチェル・ウォルツァー（アメリカ英語）
Bob Werley (AmE)　　ボブ・ワーリー（アメリカ英語）

## Life across the Waves
楽しいアメリカ生活

2016年1月20日　初版発行
2021年3月15日　第3刷発行

著　者　William A. O'Donnell
　　　　芝垣　哲夫

発行者　佐野　英一郎

発行所　株式会社 成美堂
　　　　〒101-0052　東京都千代田区神田小川町3-22
　　　　TEL 03-3291-2261　FAX 03-3293-5490
　　　　https://www.seibido.co.jp

印刷・製本　倉敷印刷㈱

ISBN 978-4-7919-4785-0　　　　　　　Printed in Japan

・落丁・乱丁本はお取り替えします。
・本書の無断複写は、著作権上の例外を除き著作権侵害となります。

# MEMO

MEMO

MEMO